level 3

UNLOCKING THE SECRETS OF PLAYING

drums

Noam Lederman
Series Creator and Supervisory Editor

Winner

Published by Winner Music Pte Ltd
707 East Coast Road
Singapore 459063
Singapore

ISBN 978-1-910762-02-8
VV00003

Series creator and supervisory editor: Noam Lederman
Written by Noam Lederman
Music engraving: Tom Fleming
Edited by Tom Fleming
Photography: Matthew Ward
Additional photography: Chiko Photography
Personality images courtesy of Corbis
Dream Theater (p. 29) courtesy of Getty Images
Cover and book design: Chloë Alexander Design
Special thanks to Theron Lim and Jai Dzafir

www.vvinner.com
www.noamlederman.com

Contents

Free Downloads

- *Graded pieces: demonstration & backing tracks*
- *Ear training exercises*

Visit **vvinner.com/downloads**

Introduction

Welcome to *Unlocking the Secrets of Playing Drums Level 3.*

This book is for every drum and beat enthusiasm around the globe. It was designed to reveal the secrets of becoming a successful drummer. The book will encourage you to develop using the most efficient learning method according to your technique. Although the book is self-explanatory and you will be able to go through it on your own, a good teacher will help make the process quicker and ensure that you do not develop any unwanted habits in the early stages.

Unlocking the Secrets of Playing Drums Level 3 covers Grades 6, 7 and 8. If you are intending on taking an earlier grade or finding the content of this book too challenging check out the *Level 1* and/or *Level 2* books in this series.

In this book we will learn about new styles of drumming and deepen our understanding of style that were taught earlier in the series.

We will also learn advanced hand and foot techniques, polyrhythms, advanced improvisation concepts and more.

Throughout the book, you will be encouraged to develop your creativity and individuality as well as exchange both your aural and reading skills in order to become the best musician you can be.

Remember that everyone learns in a different way and you will need to identify the most efficient learning method for you as an individual. This is the key to unlocking the secrets of playing drums.

I hope that you find this book useful and enjoy the journey of becoming a successful drummer.

Noam Lederman, series creator

Drum Notation

Drums

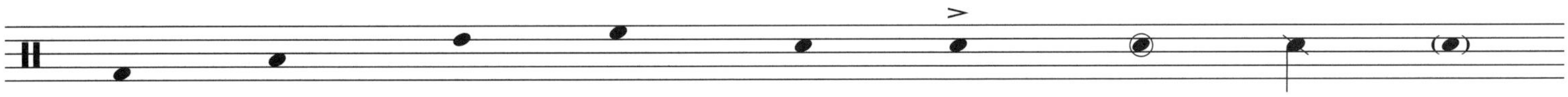

Bass Drum | Floor Tom | Mid Tom | High Tom | Snare Drum | Accent (play louder) | Cross Stick | Rimshot | Ghost Note (soft)

Cymbals

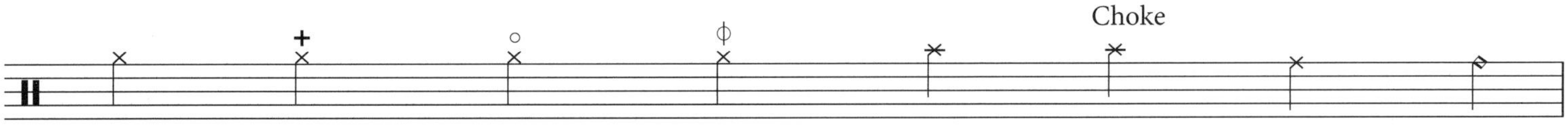

Hi-Hat (closed) | Hi-Hat (open) | Hi-Hat (half open) | Hi-Hat | Crash Cymbal | Crash (choke) | Crash Cymbal | Bell of Ride

Note & Rest Values

Notes whole (semibreve) | half (minim) | quarter (crotchet) | eighths (quavers) | eighth triplets (quaver triplets) | sixteenths (semiquavers) | sixteenth sextuplets (semiquaver sextuplets) | thirty-secondths (demisemiquavers)

Rests

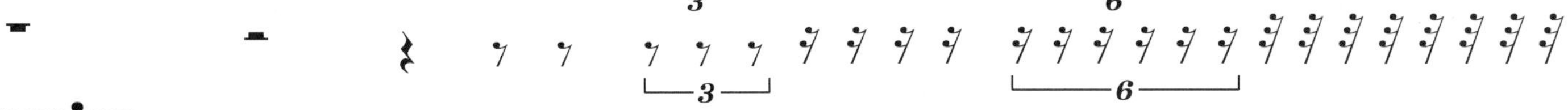

Dynamics

very soft *pp* | soft *p* | moderately soft *mp* | moderately loud *mf* | loud *f* | very loud *ff*

crescendo: get gradually louder | diminuendo: get gradually softer

Musical Structure

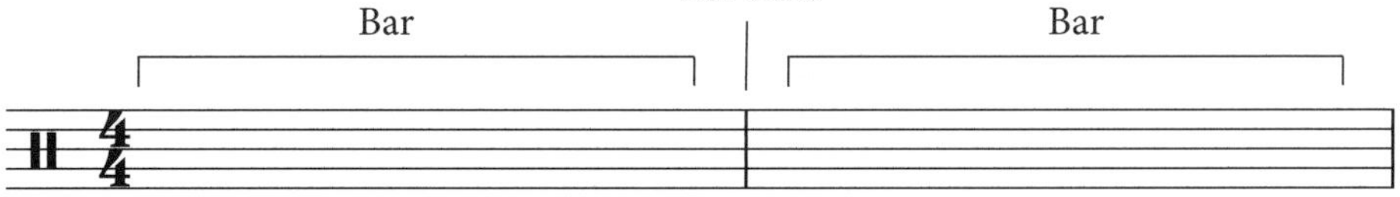

Start Repeat | Repeat everything between the repeat signs | End Repeat

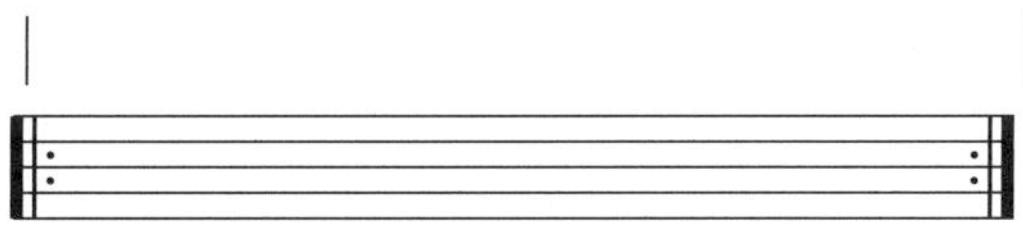

Repeat the previous bar

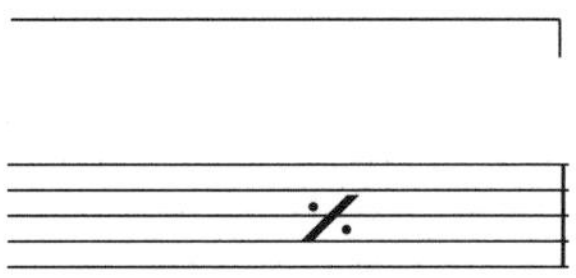

Repeat the previous 2 bars

First & second time bars:
Play the first time bar, repeat from start repeat, then go straight to the second time bar (miss the first time bar)

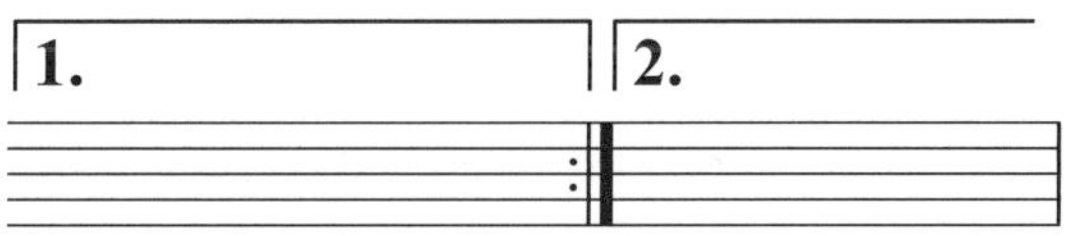

D.C. al Coda - Go back to the beginning and follow the To Coda sign

D.C. al Coda

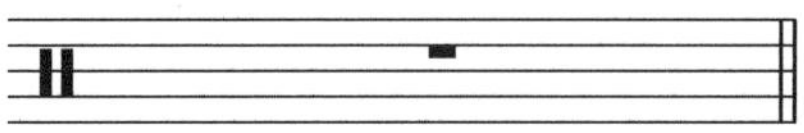

D.𝄋. al Coda – Go back to the 𝄋 sign and follow the To Coda sign

D.𝄋. al Coda

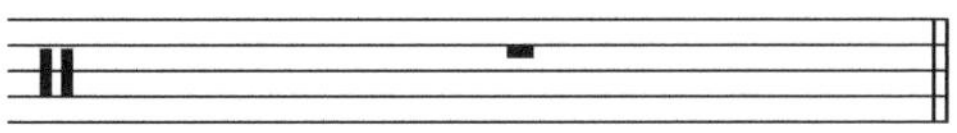

Time signature: Top number indicates the number of beats per bar.
Bottom number shows the note type used for each beat (e.g. 4/4 means 4 quarter notes per bar)

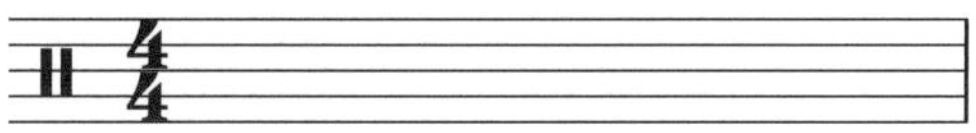

Gladstone Technique and Rudiments

Gladstone Technique

At this level we will explore advanced techniques and explain how these can be applied to your drumming. The first of these techniques is known as Controlled Strokes, or more commonly the Gladstone Technique. This technique is based on the four strokes introduced previously: the full stroke, downstroke, upstroke and the tap stroke.

These four strokes can be divided into two categories: accented strokes (full and downstroke) and unaccented strokes (upstroke and tap). Practise each stroke individually at a slow tempo until it feels comfortable.

Remember the starting point and ending point for each stroke. It is recommended to practise these on a practice pad as well as the snare drum.

First, play Exercise 1 below using each of the four strokes:

Full – high, high
Downstroke – high, low
Upstroke – low, high
Tap – low, low

1

Now, we will look at combining these four controlled strokes and applying the concept of the Gladstone technique to a single paradiddle.

Strokes will be marked as follows: **F** – full stroke, **D** – Downstroke, **U** – Upstroke, **T** – Tap stroke. Remember to reverse the sticking.

2

3

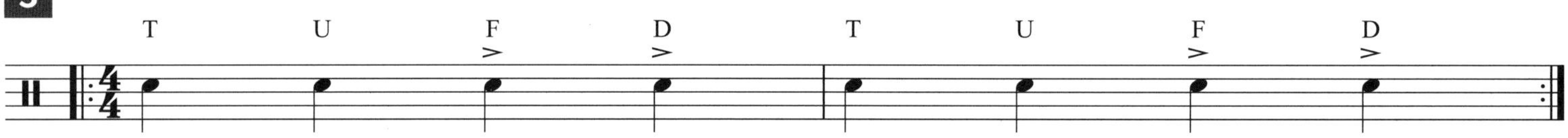

4

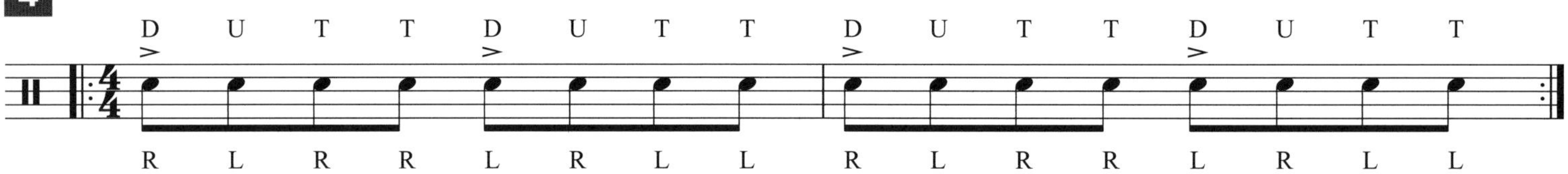

Tip!

Focus on the natural movement of the stick and do not tense any muscles while creating controlled strokes.

Rudiments

Single Ratamacue

The single ratamacue consists of a sixteenth note triplet followed by an accented eighth note. There is also a drag to perform before each triplet. The starting hand alternates so this is a great opportunity to balance and develop your stick control further. Try to apply the Gladstone technique to this rudiment for maximum accuracy.

Controlled Ruff

This is a fantastic exercise to improve accuracy and control. Begin your practice at a slow tempo and use the Gladstone Technique to ensure that the phrase is articulated clearly. This exercise is also referred to as a three stroke ruff.

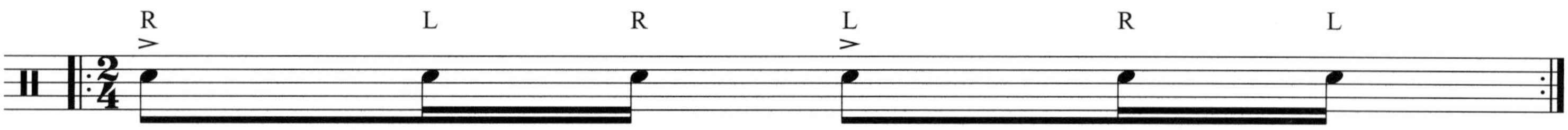

Flam Drag

Start by practising the phrase without the flams. Ensure that the double in each hand is accurate and effortless. Plan ahead so you know exactly which stroke will be used for each note. Use controlled strokes and apply slight pressure with the fulcrum when reaching high tempos.

Tip!

The fulcrum in drumming means the grip of the stick by the thumb and index fingers. At this advanced stage of your drumming, you should notice that minor adjustments to the fulcrum can improve your technique and allow you to play faster and louder effortlessly.

Advanced Bass Drum Techniques

To reach full potential with the bass drum it is important to understand, practise and integrate various techniques into your playing.

Heel Down

Keep your foot flat on the pedal and allow the beater to come off the drum head after the stroke. Play consistent eighth notes at various speeds and dynamic levels until this feels comfortable. Next, integrate this into the grooves, fills and solos that you already know how to play. This technique is primarily used when playing softer styles of music.

Heel Up

Keep your heel up throughout and feel your whole leg moving up and down. This technique uses the biggest motion and therefore produces the loudest sound.

Heel Up & Down

Lift the heel up slightly and angle the foot inwards a little. Ensure that the action is initiated and performed with the heel up but between strokes allow the foot to be in the heel down position. This technique is very useful when playing for long periods of time.

Heel Toe

This technique is also known as the Constant Release Technique and is associated with the drummer Freddie Gruber. In this technique you alternate between Heel Up and Heel Down to create fluent motion and consistently fast strokes. This is similar to the stick control rebound motion (Moeller Technique) and can be developed into motions and phrases of two, three, four and even five. This technique is advanced and may take months to learn. Watching videos of drummers perform this technique correctly could be very helpful in the early stages (Steve Smith, Jojo Mayer).

In the Exercises 1–3 there are constant strokes on the bass drum. Practise these with all four of the techniques discussed above and aim to gradually improve all of them. Do not focus on speed. Practise slowly and allow your body to understand and memorise the correct movement.

Exercise 4 combines all four bass drum techniques: Heel Down for the first time, on the second Heel Up, on the third, Heel Up and Down and on the fourth Heel Toe. When you reach the end, start over again. If you prefer, you can start by only mixing two of the techniques and keep alternating until you feel ready to attempt the complete exercise.

1

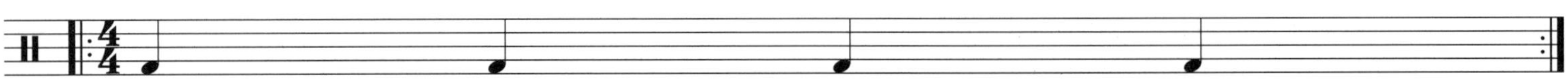

2

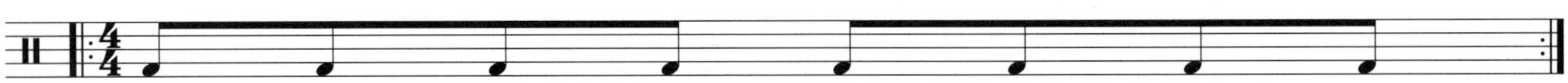

3

4

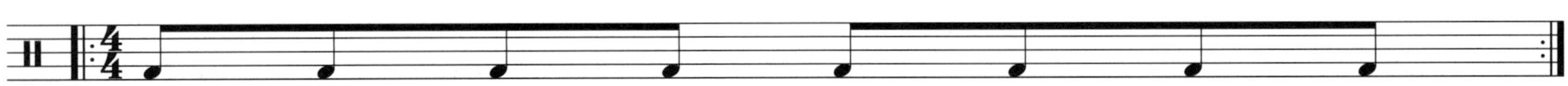

1. Heel Down 2. Heel Up 3. Heel Up and Down 4. Heel Toe

Fast Doubles

This is a very effective technique for playing two consecutive bass drum notes at high tempos, based on using the natural rebound of the drum head, and is similar in concept to the rebound hand technique where we are using one move to create multiple strokes. In this case, we are aiming to create two even strokes with one move. This is often referred to as the slide technique.

Set yourself in the Heel Up position and pull your foot back so your toes are just over the half point of the pedal board. Play one stroke, follow the natural rebound of the pedal and then slide your foot up to create the second stroke with minimum effort. When you understand this technique you will realise that it can significantly increase your doubles speed and is well worth practising. This can obviously be used in any style of music and it is a very important tool.

1

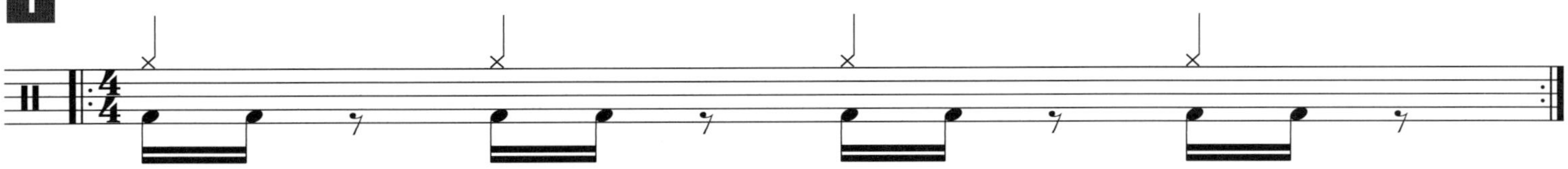

2

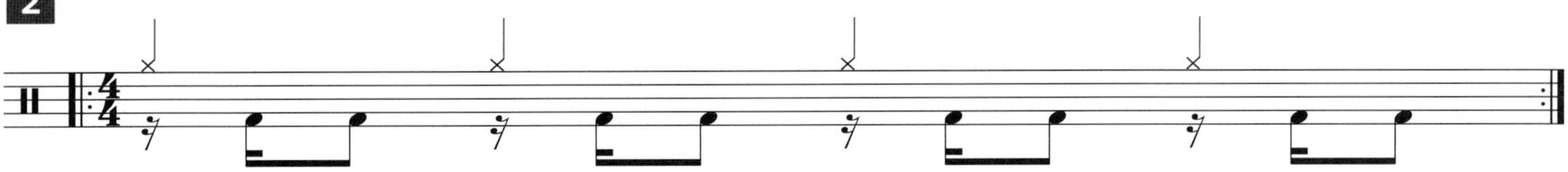

3

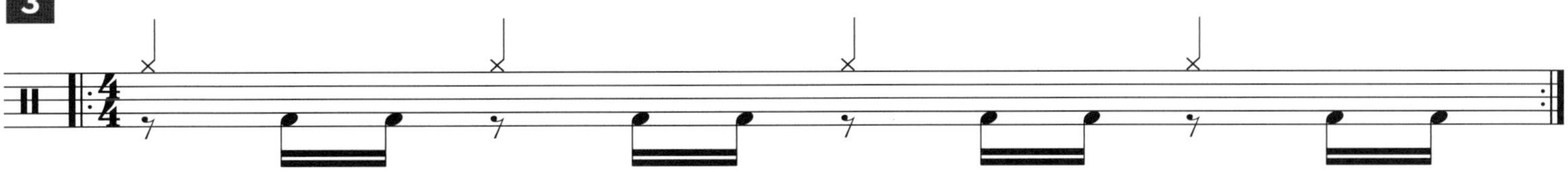

Slide Technique Phrases

These phrases test your understanding of this technique. Practise these daily and keep track of your speed. Set weekly tempo targets and keep improving until this becomes a natural part of your drumming.

> **Tip!**
>
> *Some drummers prefer to angle the foot on the pedal slightly before the slide and straighten it for second stroke. This is also a very effective version of the slide technique.*

4

5

6

Cross-Sticking

The cross-sticking motion occurs when we lift one hand above the other in order to reach a certain drum. Using cross-sticking during fills will help you achieve any drum voicing you desire regardless of your hands position.

This technique is also very visually impressive and will therefore add flair to your showmanship. The exercises below will explore how this technique can be used. Cross-sticking motions are marked with a circle around the striking hand: Ⓛ Ⓡ

1

2

3

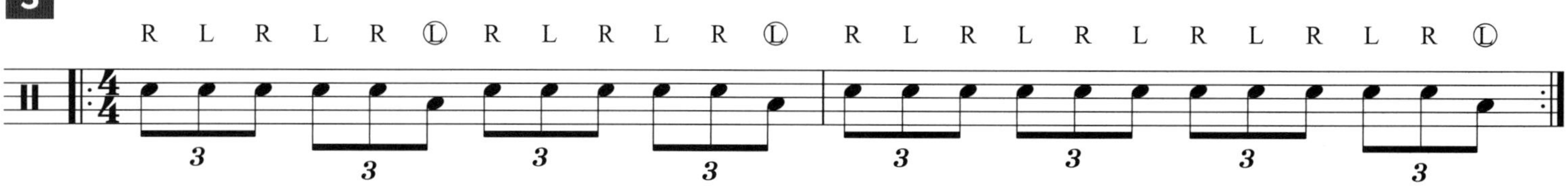

4

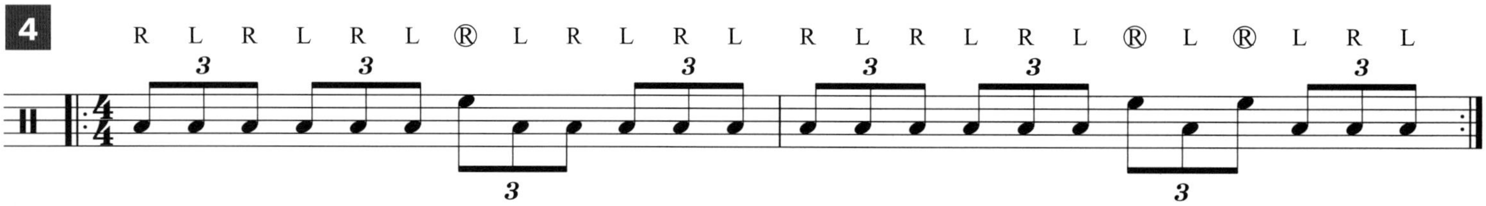

Tip!

It is important to maintain good posture when performing this technique and not compensate with any unnecessary movements. Remember to stay relaxed and allow your hands to move freely and with ease. If you feel you are straining any part of your body, take a break, stretch and try again.

Cross-Sticking Fills

Here are six slightly more complex phrases using cross-sticking. These can be used as fills or in solos.

1

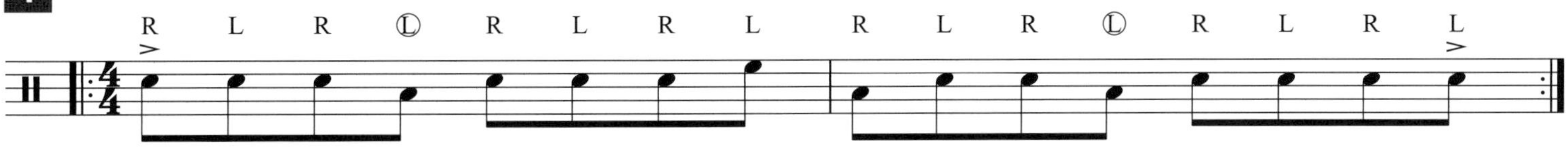

2

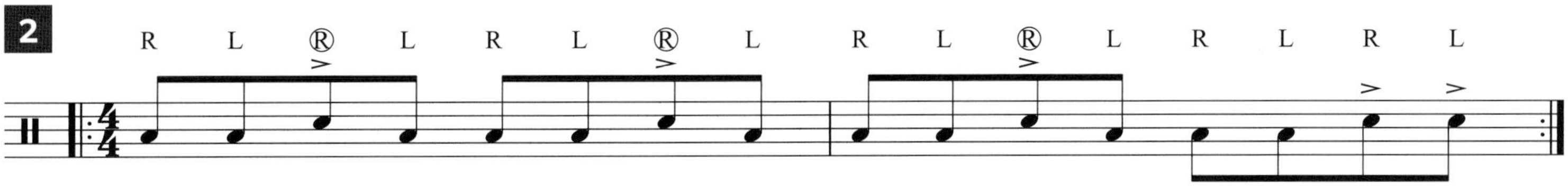

3

4

5

6

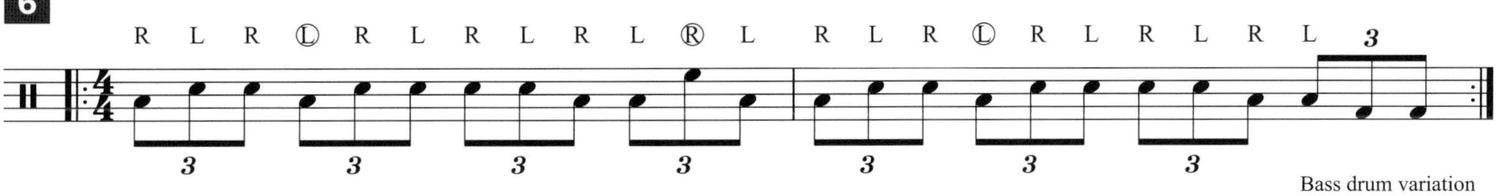

Four-Way Coordination

Developing your four-way coordination is an integral part of improving your overall control of the instrument. Although practising exercises of this type can seem boring at first, once you get into it and your coordination improves you will enjoy feeling the benefits. Remember that this is not about speed, so focus on achieving the most efficient, accurate and effortless movement with each limb. Maintain a balanced posture and stay relaxed.

This four-way coordination concept develops the ability to combine and play various musical parts simultaneously. We will refer to these musical parts as: patterns **A** and patterns **B**. Patterns A1-A4 below include rhythmic phrases that should initially be played with the bass drum. Each pattern from page 13 (B1-B5) should be played constantly while going through the A1-A5 patterns. The idea is to create and play all possible variations from combining the A and B patterns. This will immensely improve your control and movement around the kit.

Aim to alternate between any of the A and B patterns without stopping. Then you can create your own variations and continue to practise on the kit. Remember that this is only the first step. In order to take it further, all limbs need to be able to play the A patterns while the B patterns are played with an additional drum voice such as the hi-hat foot.

A1

A2

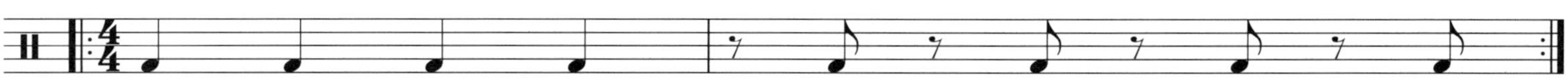

A3

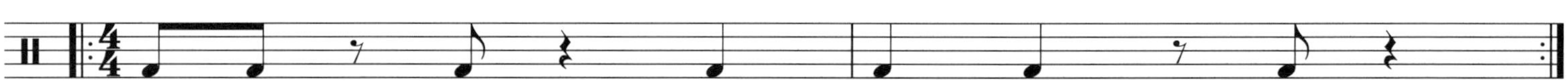

A4

These five patterns should be used with the A patterns shown in the previous page. Focus on the points where drum voices are played in unison (together) and use these as the anchor for the groove. Then, concentrate on adding the more challenging patterns.

B1

Hi-Hat Groove

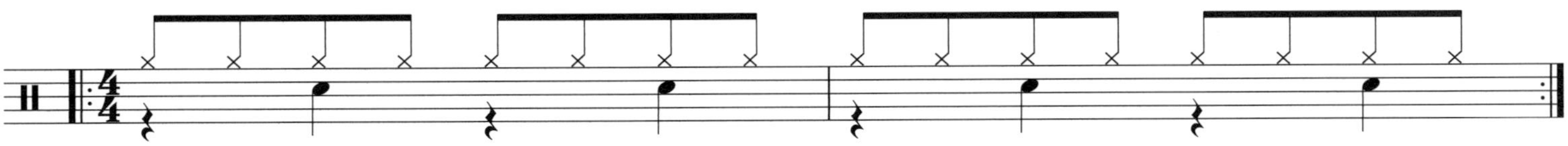

B2

Hi-Hat/SD Paradiddle

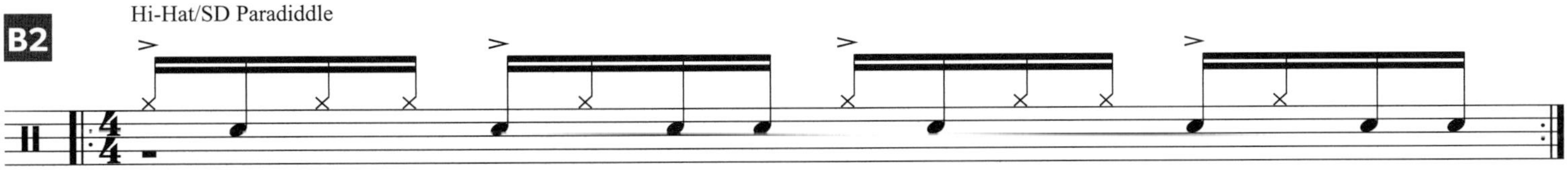

B3

Hi-Hat 16s and Cross Stick

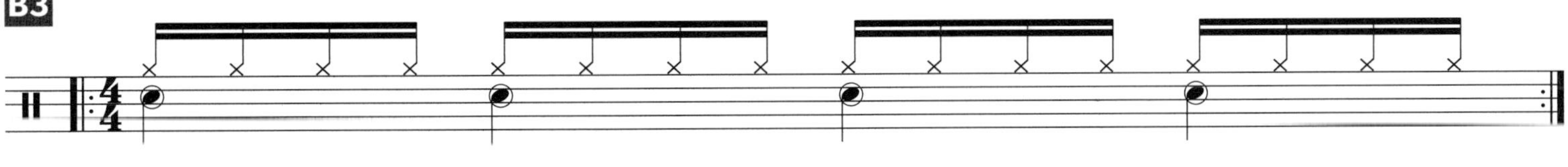

B4

Bell Ride Variation

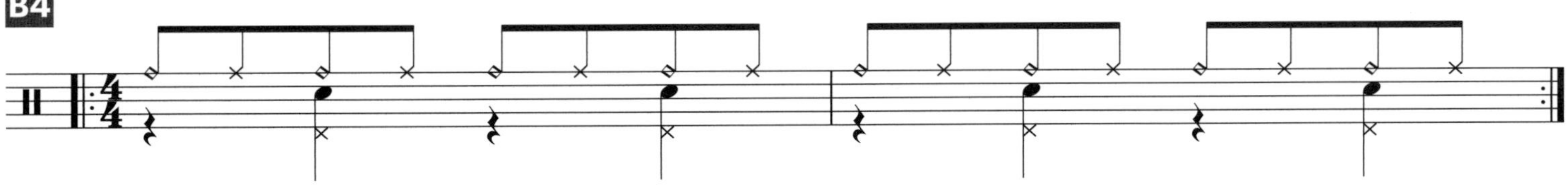

B5

Ride Groove With Hi-Hat Foot

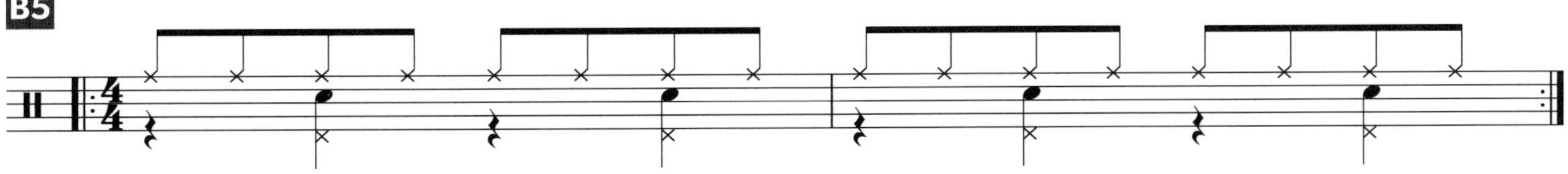

Drumming in Five

In this lesson you will learn about grooves in odd time signatures. These will not follow the standard $\frac{4}{4}$ time signature, but focus on five quarter notes instead: one extra beat. Later in this lesson we will also learn about grooves in $\frac{5}{8}$ which means five eighth notes per bar. Although we will focus on rock beats in five, it is important to remember that any of these grooves can be slightly modified to suit different musical styles with odd time signatures, including African music, Latin, jazz and many more.

As with all odd time signatures, it is important to understand the rhythms and count the beats. The phrase of five can always be divided into 3+2 or 2+3 depending on the musical context. Practise the grooves below with a metronome and keep counting until you feel comfortable with the cycle of five. Feel free to add fills to the $\frac{5}{4}$ grooves as well as your own groove variations.

1

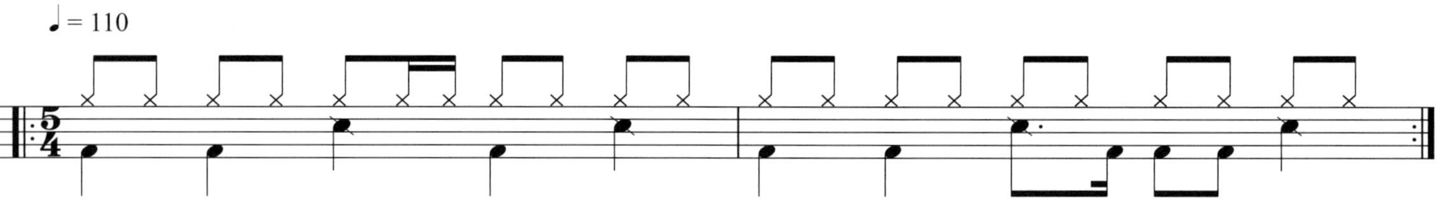

2

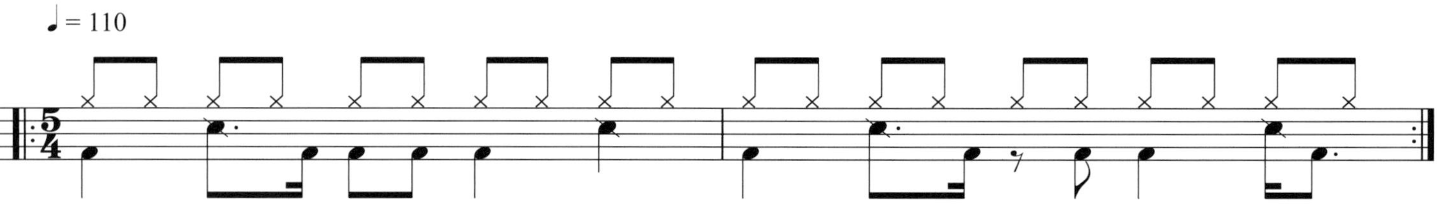

3

Try playing one bar of the odd time signature followed by one bar of $\frac{4}{4}$. This is a good way of learning odd time signatures and also leads to musical and interesting combinations of time signatures such as the following example, which is effectively in $\frac{9}{4}$.

4

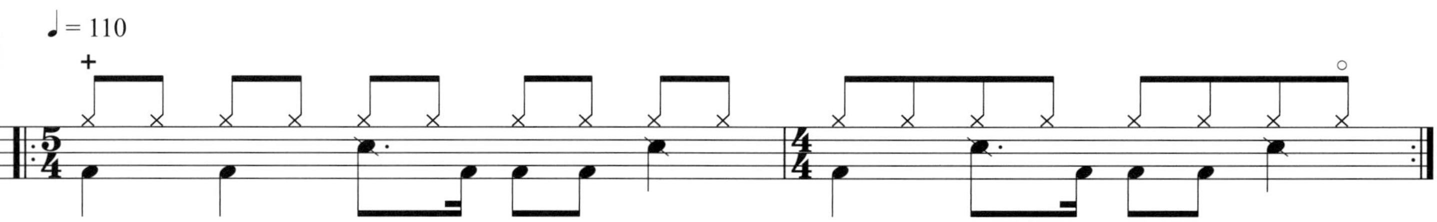

5/8 Grooves

Now let's try some grooves in 5/8. The same concept applies but this time we are counting in eighth notes.

1

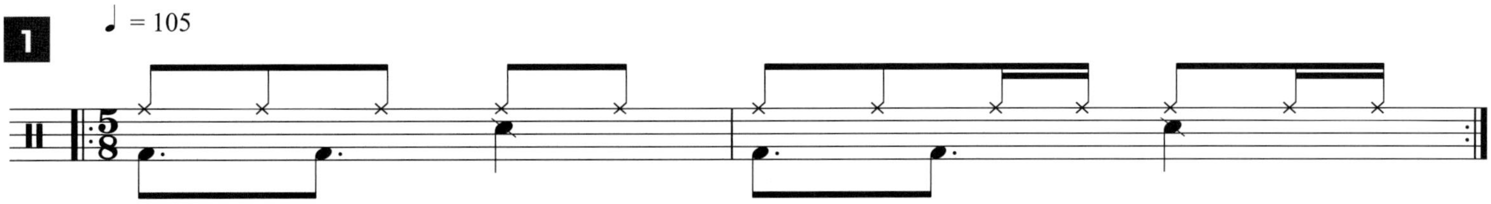

2

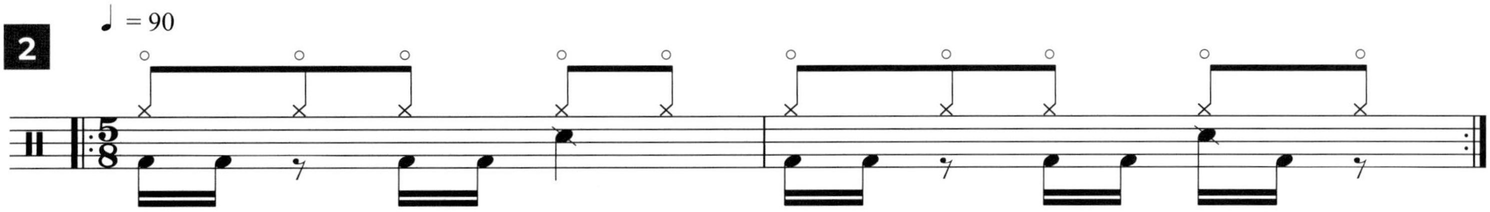

In the following groove we will introduce a challenging and highly effective concept for odd time signatures. In this concept the bass drum and snare are clearly playing the 5/8 groove with the hi-hat playing consistent eighth notes.

By adding alternate accents to the hi-hat pattern, we can create an interesting combination of rhythms that sounds intricate to the listener. Practise this with careful attention to the accents and ensure it does not feel rushed.

3

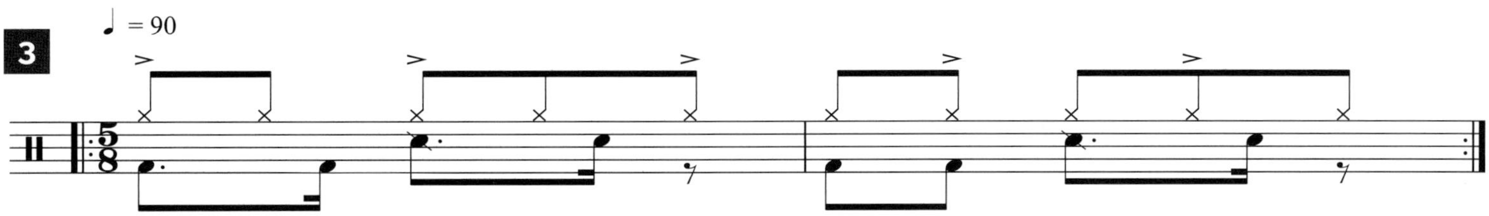

5/8 Fills

Here are a few examples for fills in 5/8. The more comfortable you feel with this time signature the easier it will be to adapt your favourite fills to it.

> **Tip!**
>
> *Check out these tracks in five:*
> - *Dave Brubeck: 'Take Five'*
> - *Sting: 'Seven Days'*
> - *Radiohead: '15 Step'*

4

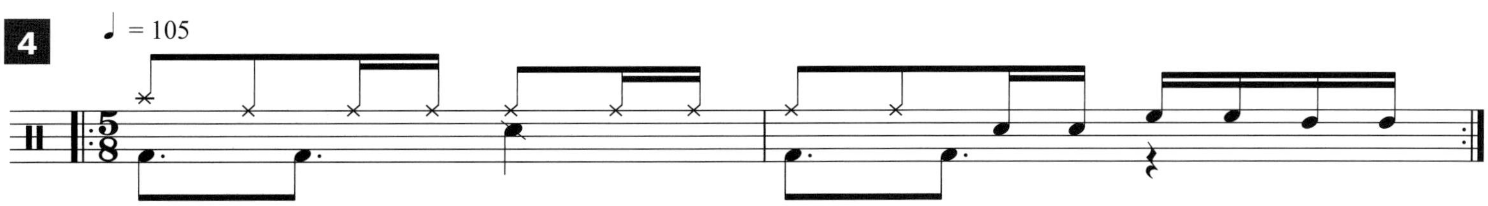

5

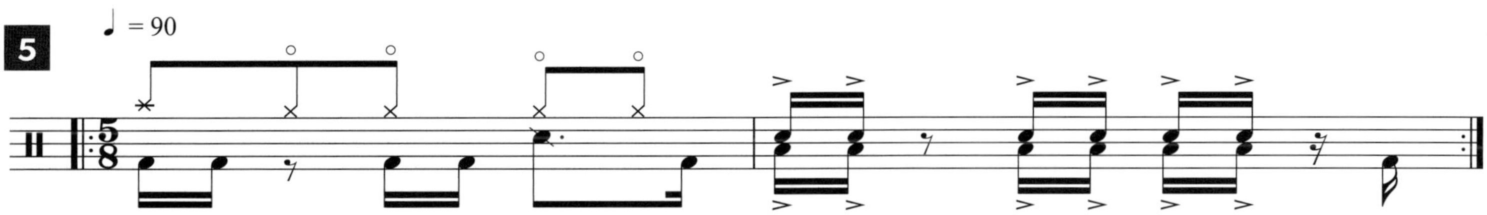

Advanced Rhythms

Thirty-Second Notes

Thirty-second notes are the next subdivision of the quarter beat after sixteenth notes. A thirty-second note is equal to half a sixteenth note and is also known as a demisemiquaver.

Practise the exercises below with the hands playing the thirty-second notes both in singles and doubles. Aim to achieve accurate, focused and balanced strokes throughout.

1

2

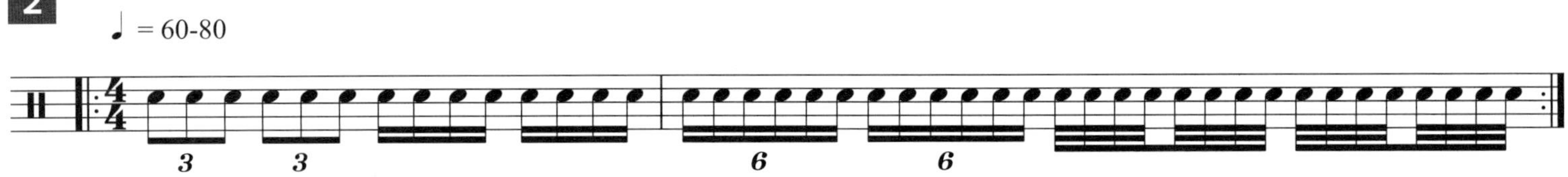

3

The thirty-second rest (𝅀) is equal to half a sixteenth note rest. Let's look at exercises that include thirty-second rests.

4

5

Quintuplets

This lesson introduces groups of five even sixteenth strokes that are equal to one quarter note beat. These are known as quintuplets. Start by practising consistent quintuplets in order to understand the rhythm and the speed of the notes. If you are unsure whether you are playing quintuplets correctly, play sixteenth notes for a few bars, then sixteenth note sextuplets for a few bars. The quintuplets should be exactly in the middle of those two rhythms. When you feel ready, try the exercises below on the snare drum. You will see that if you follow alternate sticking the hand that lands on the beat will change every time. This is because the quintuplets have an odd number of notes.

1

♩ = 60-80

2

♩ = 60-80

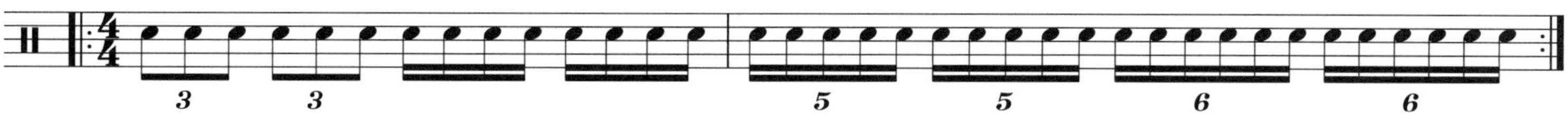

Septuplets

Dividing a quarter note beat by seven results in septuplets. Follow alternate sticking and be aware that the leading hand on each beat will change, as when playing quintuplets. The speed of the strokes should be between sextuplets (six strokes per beat) and thirty-second notes (eight strokes per beat). Once you feel comfortable with this rhythm try the exercises below.

3

♩ = 60-80

4

♩ = 60-80

Hip Hop

In this lesson we will explore hip hop grooves. The five exercises notated below will give you an inspiring glimpse into these cool grooves.

Ex. 1: This is a sixteenth note hip hop groove with one thirty second note rest and one thirty-second note played on the hi-hat. The right hand plays the hi-hat pattern throughout.

Ex. 2: In this groove we have a complex rhythmic phrase on the fourth beat. It includes the cross stick sound that was learnt earlier in this series and another new stylistic sound. This sound is produced by hitting the stick that is held by the left hand with the stick that is held by the right hand. This sound will be marked with '*' in the notation below

Ex. 3: The hi-hat pattern in this groove is played by the right hand only. Keep this relaxed so you will be able to play the thirty-second notes with ease.

Ex. 4: Use both hands to play the fast thirty-second note phrase on the hi-hat.

Ex. 5: This is a hip hop groove with a triplet jazz feel in the style of Chris 'Daddy' Dave and Questlove.

1

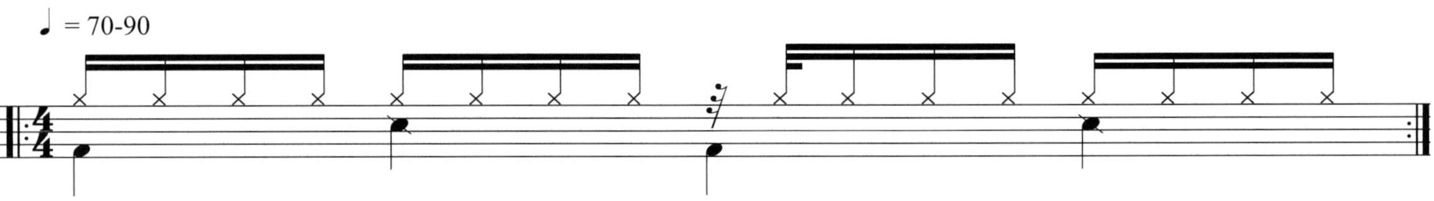

2

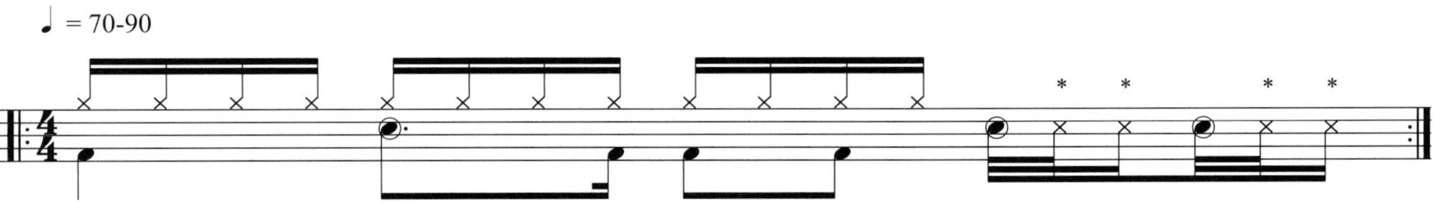

3

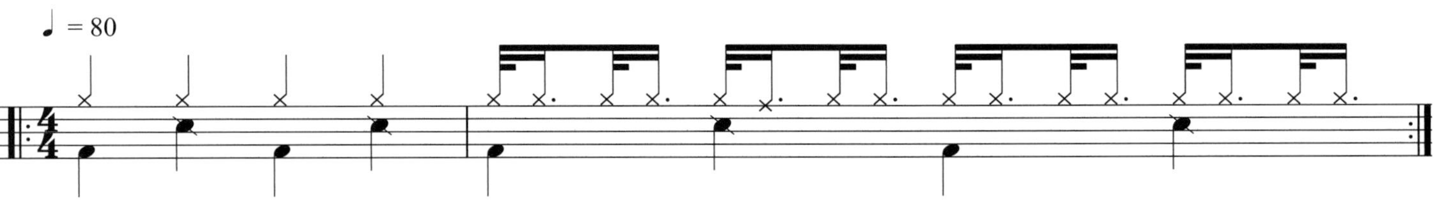

4

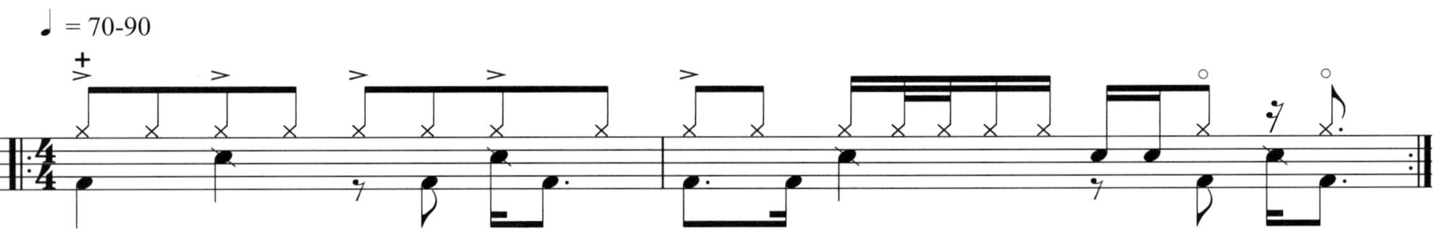

5

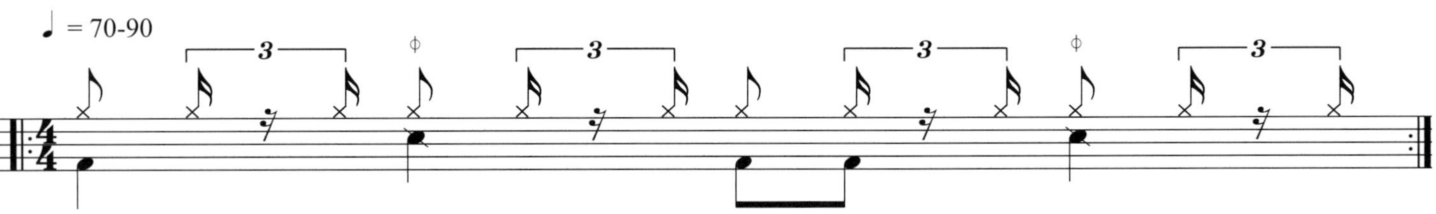

Claps

The backbeat clap is an important sound in the hip hop language. There are a few ways to re-create this electronic sound on the acoustic drum kit. Three of these are shown below.

Ex. 1: Right hand plays main stroke as cross stick, left hand plays grace note on rim of snare.

Ex. 2: Right hand plays the hi-hat throughout, left hand slides from hi tom rim to cross stick snare.

Ex. 3: Right hand plays hi-hat and snare side rim grace note. Left hand slides from high tom rim to cross stick snare.

Ex. 4: Right hand plays the hi-hat pattern and rim shot snare. Left hand plays cross stick. Aim for a consistent sound between the hi-hat foot and right hand hi-hats.

1

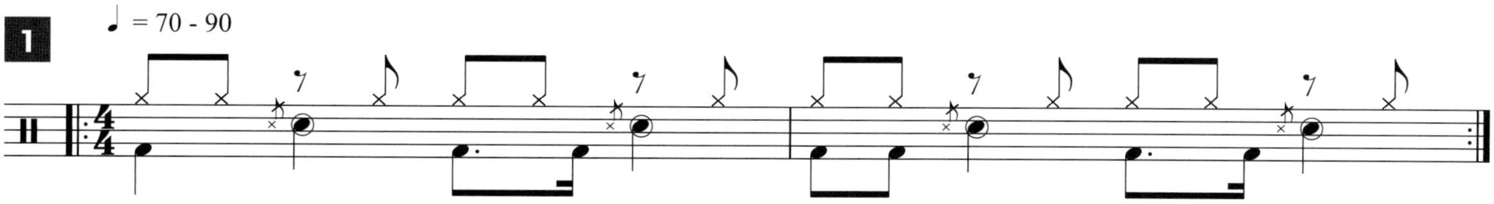

2

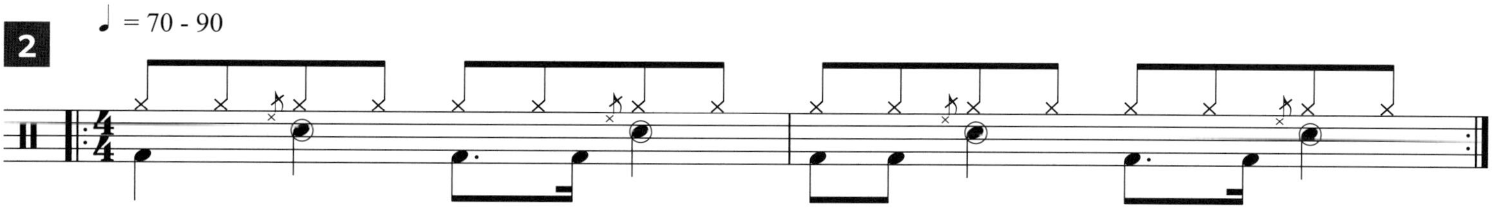

3

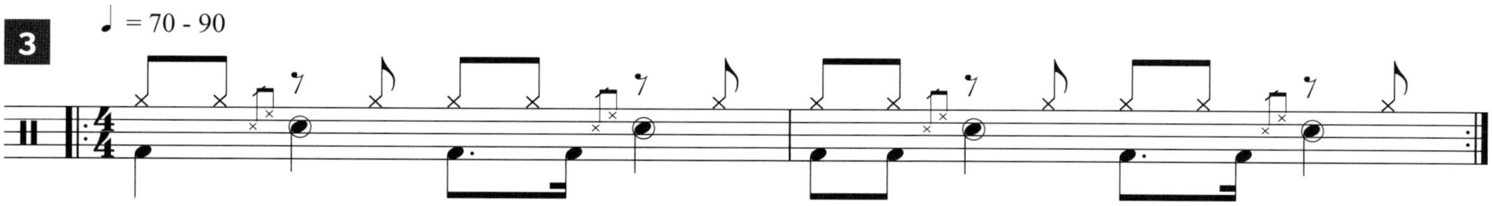

4

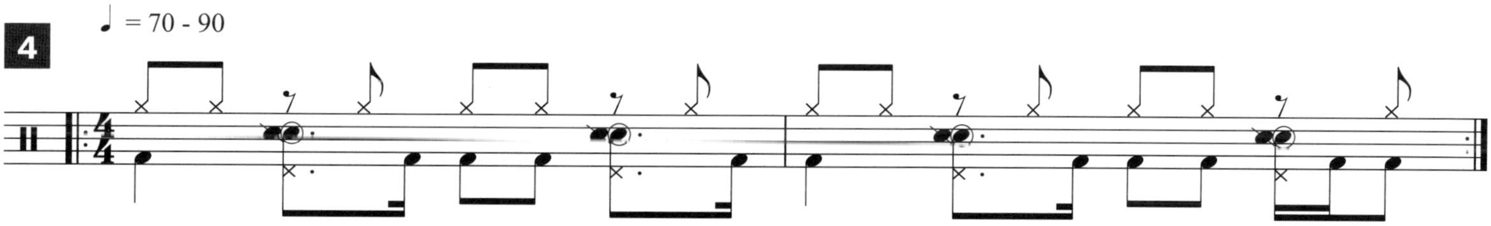

Tip!

Check out these hip hop drummers:
Questlove
Chris 'Daddy' Dave
Adam Deitch
Tony Roster, Jr.
Gerald Heyward
Kenton Bostick
Mark Colenburg

Samba

Samba grooves as played on the drum kit are adapted from the patterns of Brazilian percussion instruments such as surdo, pandeiro, tamborim, repinique, cuica and agogô. Samba is usually notated in $\frac{2}{4}$.

Ex. 1: A traditional samba pattern on the hi-hat with bass drum emphasis on the second beat. This emphasis imitates the backbeat provided by the surdo (traditional samba drum).

Ex. 2: This is the most common samba feet pattern. Get comfortable with this before going on to **Ex. 3–5**.

Ex. 3: Samba groove on the hi-hat with the traditional bass drum pattern.

Ex. 4: Samba feet with samba pattern on snare with accents and rim shots. You can replace any rim shot with a buzz roll to achieve a stylistic variation.

Ex. 5: Snare and toms samba pattern.

1

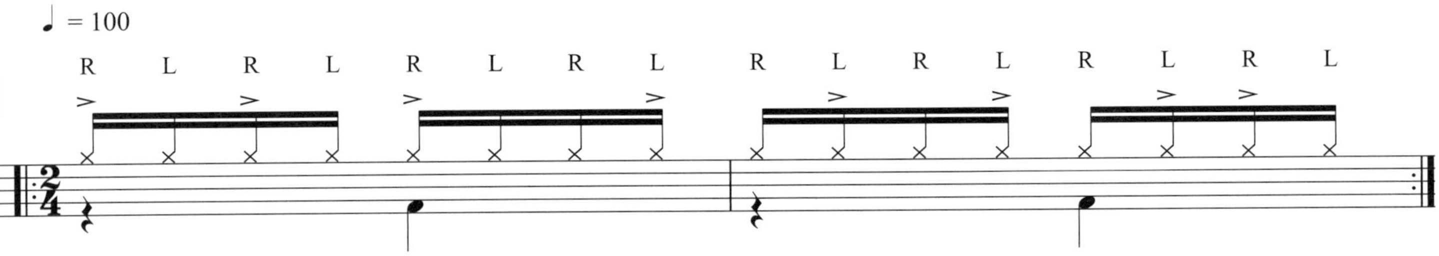

2

3

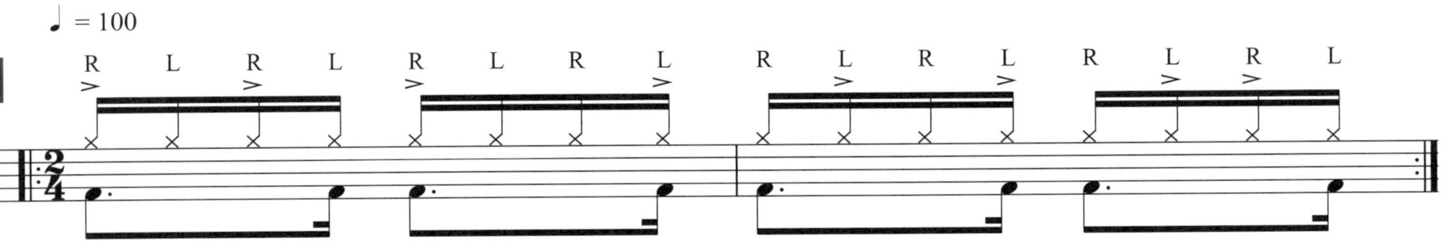

4

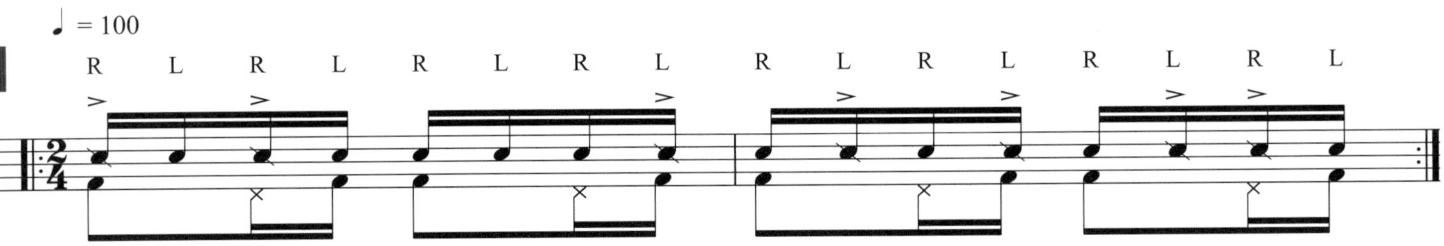

5

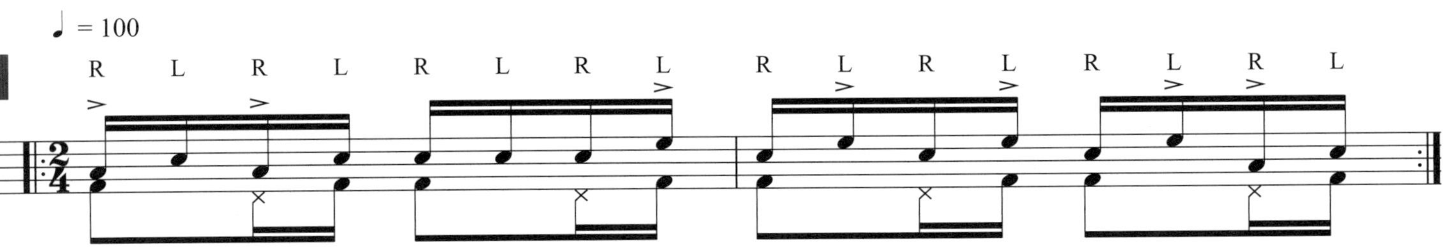

Splashed Hi-Hat

The exercises below involve straight eighth notes with the hi-hat foot. The splashed hi-hat sound is created by lifting the ankle and hitting the bottom of the hi- hat pedal plate so that the cymbals hit each other.

The splashed hi-hat in the following exercises is marked with a circle under the hi-hat foot note. These samba patterns are effective at many tempos.

Follow your own technical ability and choose your own practice speed.

1

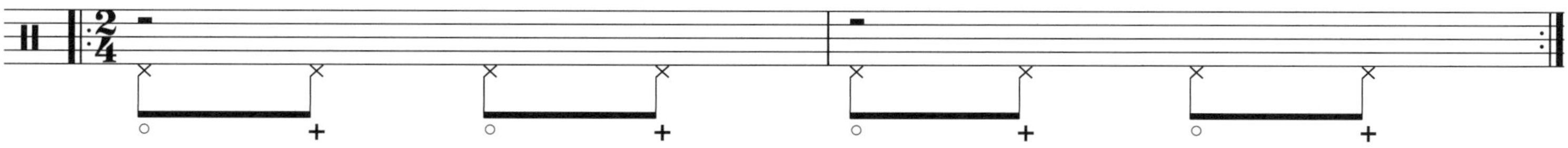

2

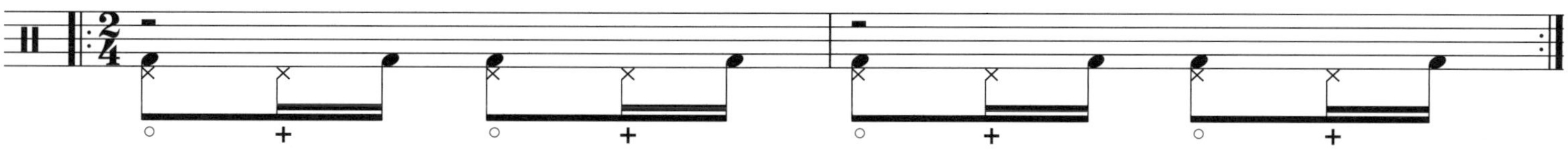

3

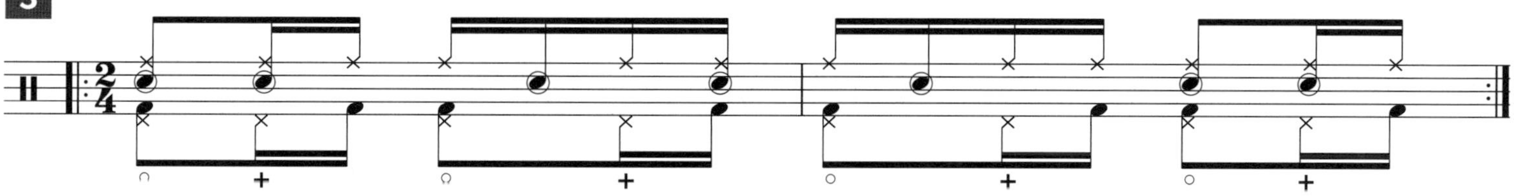

Closed Floor Tom

The closed floor tom sound is another stylistic technique in samba. You can create this by hitting the floor tom with the stick and keeping the tip of the stick in contact with the drumhead in order to dampen the sound. The pattern constantly changes between these closed (damped) and open (non-damped) sounds.

The closed sound is notated with '+' in the exercises below. We will show you how to incorporate this with a traditional samba groove in **Ex. 5**. If you want to challenge yourself try combining **Ex. 5** with the splashed hi-hat technique shown above.

4

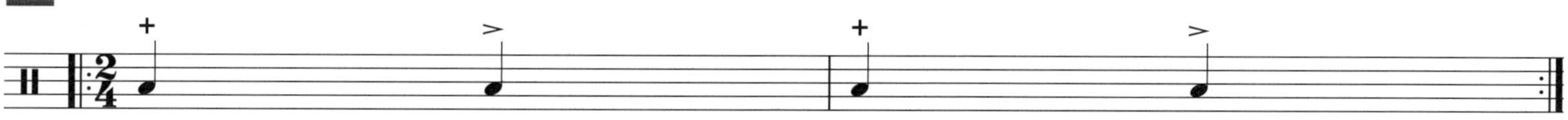

5

Musicianship

Playing Live

Being a professional musician is much more than just playing the fastest ever paradiddle around the drum kit. It requires dedication, understanding of the market, and many elements that young musicians tend to forget when planning to conquer the music world. At this grade we will explore the most important points to think of when starting to perform live. We will look into other aspects of musicianship later in this book.

First and foremost, you have to ensure that your drumming is up to scratch. You should be able to play various grooves with good time and feel, read notation, improvise, listen, solo and gel with other musicians with ease. If you are struggling with any of these elements, create additional daily practice time and deal with them. Your drumming is your craft and a regular practise regime is the only way to ensure that you are progressing in your art.

Equipment

When thinking of equipment for live gigs, we need to consider a few points:

- What type of gig is it? (original, function, TV.)
- What is the venue? (large hall, reception room.)
- How many people will attend?
- How big is the band?
- What style(s) of music will you be playing?
- Will there be notation for you to follow or will you be required to play by ear?
- Does the venue have a drum kit?

Knowing these details will help you decide what equipment to bring and help you mentally prepare for the challenge.

Your main contact for the gig, whether it's the musical director or one of the other musicians, should know the answers to most of these questions.

Tip!

If you are unsure what equipment to bring to a certain gig, always bring more rather than less. When you arrive at the venue, take ten minutes to scope it out properly. This will help you decide exactly the equipment that is required for the gig.

Follow this check list before leaving to a gig – this will build a healthy routine for you as a gigging musician.

1 Ensure that your drums, cymbals and hardware are packed well so they are not damaged during transport.

2 Drums should be roughly tuned in case there is not much time to tune before the gig. And don't forget your tuning key.

3 Have one spare top head for each drum (especially the snare drum).

4 Have your stick bag with plenty of spares as well as brushes, hot rods and any other sticks you like using.

5 Take a metronome for reference.

6 Make sure you always have a drum mat. This is so important as many venues have a wooden floor which will not hold your kit parts in place.

7 Music stand.

8 Any electronics that you use.

Networking

OK, so you are a solid drummer. You have prepared all your equipment and the hardware is shining, but how do you find gigs?
The answer is making contacts and networking. It is important to understand that gig offers can come from many different places. These include:

- Music venues
- Other musicians
- Musical directors
- Music producers
- Event managers
- Other venues
- Anyone that knows you

Aim to develop as many contacts as possible and make people aware that you are available for work. Going to other people's gigs and jam sessions is a great way to get yourself known and meet new musicians. Nurture the relationships you make and ensure that you do not pester anyone regarding finding work. Focus on improving your craft and making people aware who you are. Do not worry - if they like your playing they will find you.

You can also take a more active approach and contact the venue directly to find out if there is an option for you to play there. Many venues will prefer to deal with an agent so find out who are the most successful agents and agencies in your area and approach them with your profile (also referred to as 'show reel' in the music industry). If you do not have many contacts in the music scene, joining one or more agencies that will present your profile online is a good idea. They will probably be able to get you work relatively quickly. However, remember that there is a price for this service, so ensure that you are happy with the agent's commission before starting to work together.

Remember that this is a long term strategy, and if you want to work as a professional musician for life you need patience. Hopefully you will become successful and have the pleasure of playing live with many different musicians in endless musical situations. Some of the contacts that you make this year might only lead to work in three years' time but that is absolutely fine: just keep networking with other working musicians and creating more new contacts.

Social Media

Having your own web site is crucial in this business. Updating and demonstrating your various skills will help you to gain credibility. Social media can be another very important tool. When making new contacts, you will most likely be asked for your Facebook name rather than your phone number. Again, this is a good way of making your network larger by using social media but it must be done wisely.

Your online profile should represent the professional musician that you are. Therefore, ensure that the photos and videos represented as part of your profile actually show that. Any evidence of you playing with other musicians or doing anything musical that you are proud of is good to have online.

The various social media platforms also allow you to create events and maintain basic communication with your network. This is an effective way of reminding people that you exist (and that you are the right person for this gig they have...). However, it is not enough if you want to develop contacts above this basic level. Promoting yourself online and using social media should never be a replacement for going out and meeting people.

Putting It All Together

Don't treat this advice as the only guide for a working musician. As always you need to find your way to do things, and you need to be happy with what you are doing or people around you will be uncomfortable.

The process of promoting yourself, making new contacts and finding gigs can actually be a lot of fun. Just relax, take a deep breath, be yourself and get out there!

Rhythmic Soloing

It's time to explore the idea of soloing further.

Let's focus on the concept of rhythmic soloing. This type of soloing involves mixing various rhythms to express your ideas. We will look into more advanced soloing methods later in this book.

Here is a simple process you can follow to develop original rhythmic phrases. This is only one example and you may also find other ways of developing your rhythmic soloing.

1 Choose two or more rhythms that you want to combine. Play each one of them consistently around the kit, trying to find musical phrases and interpretations. When you feel comfortable with the rhythms, create a two-bar phrase that you like with them.

2 Add rests to give the phrase a more musical shape.

3 Add accents for greater expression.

4 Replace some of the notes played with the hands with the bass drum or hi-hat foot.

5 Use different sticking, stick control techniques and rudiments to create new ideas.

1

2

3

4

5

Now let's apply the rhythmic soloing concept to the two-bar phrases on this page. Remember to practise these at various tempos, apply different stylistic contexts and use the steps suggested on the previous page.

To take this concept further try to develop rhythmic phrases from songs that you like into your own solos. You can also experiment with moving the phrases around the kit but this concept will be thoroughly explained in *Melodic Soloing* (p. 54–55).

1

2

3

4

5

6

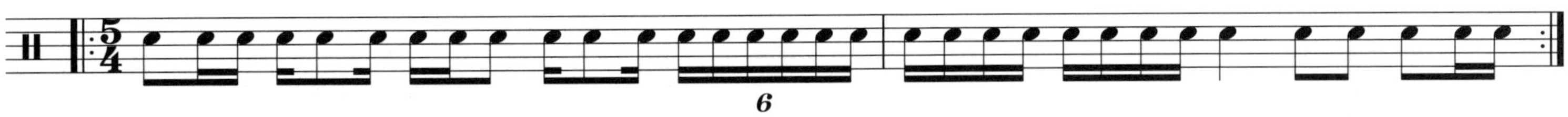

Repeated phrases are central to soloing and to drumming in general. Practise the phrase you have developed repeatedly and continue to adjust until you feel happy with the result.

Next, start creating variations on every repeat until it sounds like a solo rather than a repeated phrase. With this idea in mind, create longer solos and use the metronome to ensure that the pulse remains consistent.

Ear Training

Play each audio track without looking at the examples below.

After a count-in of four clicks, the two-bar backing is played four times. For the first and third times, listen to the recorded drums. For the second and fourth times, try to play back what you heard.

Finally, refer to the notation below to check whether you recognised the time signature, played back the exercise accurately and understand how it is written.

Exercises

1 ♩= 70

2 ♩= 70

3 ♩= 70

The following three exercises use the same rhythms as those above but with the toms as well as the snare drum. The practice concept is the same.

4 ♩= 70

5 ♩= 70

6 ♩= 70

Grooves

You will notice that Exercises 1–3 are groove based. This means that more parts of the drum kit will be used. This requires secure aural understanding as you will not only have to recognise the rhythms but also the drum voices that are being played.

As explained previously, the backing track will play four times and you should attempt to play back during the second and fourth plays. We will focus on $\frac{4}{4}$, $\frac{5}{4}$ and $\frac{5}{8}$ in these grooves, but feel free to create your own exercises in other time signatures too.

1

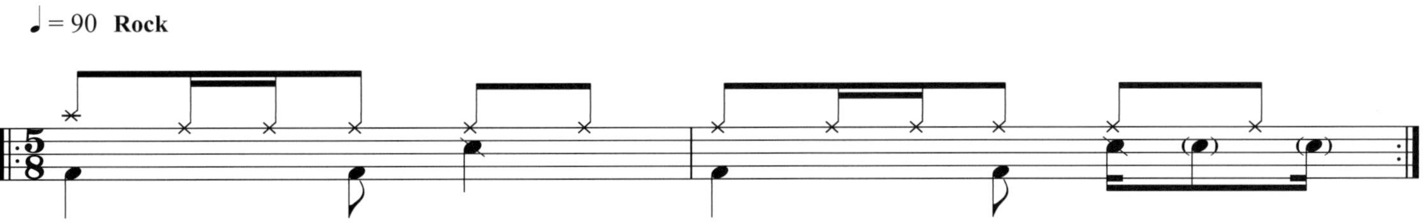

2

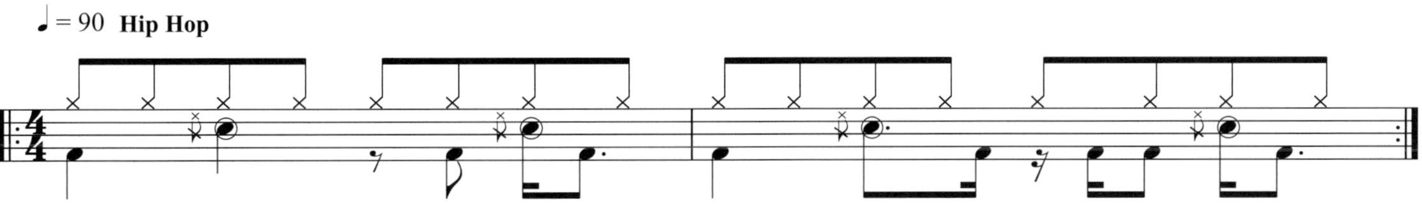

3

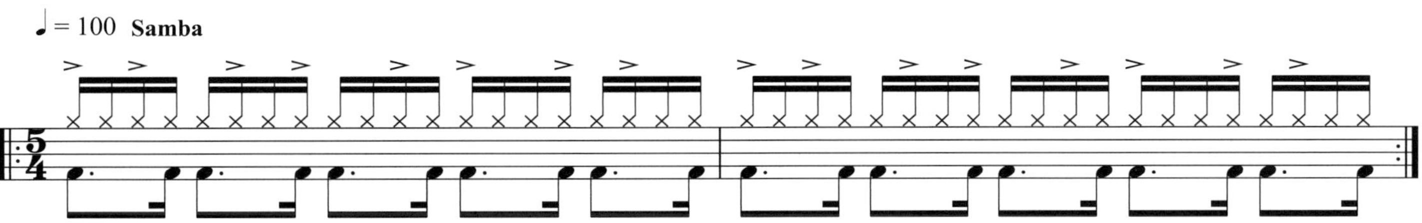

Now let's take two bar grooves and place a two beat fill at the end of the phrase. See if you can identify all the detail and play them back with conviction.

4

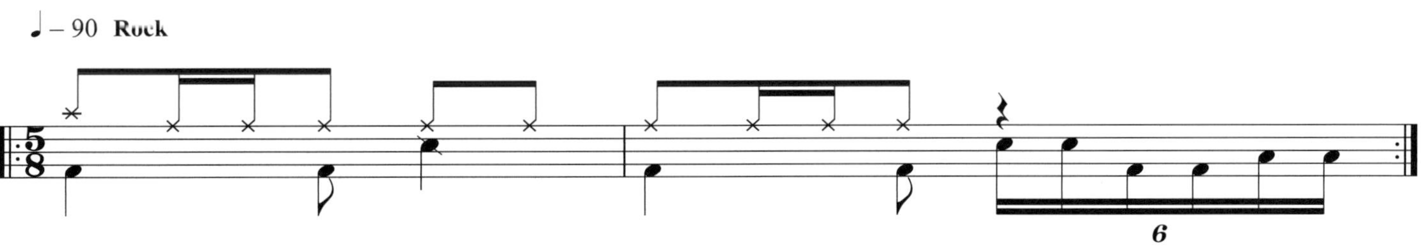

5

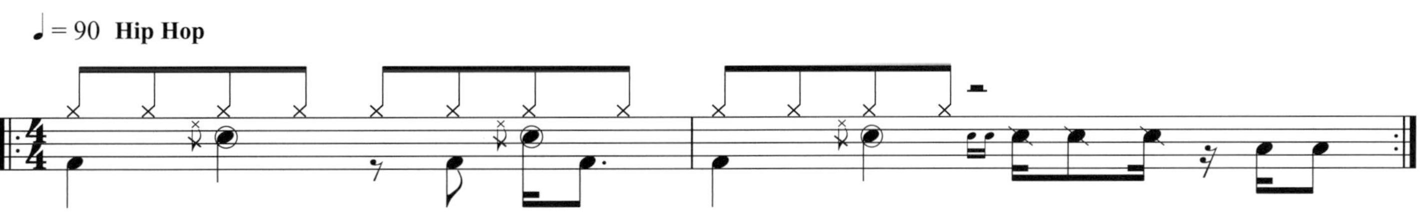

6

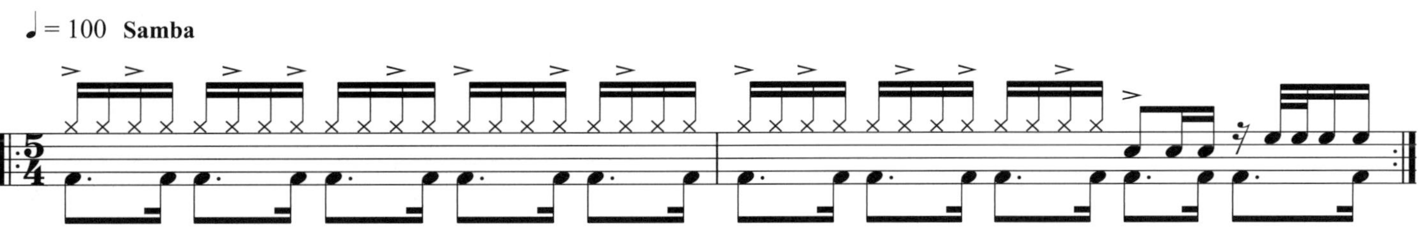

Inspirational Drummers

Mike Portnoy

Mike Portnoy is the co-founder and former drummer of the progressive rock band Dream Theater. During his 25 years and many albums with the band, Mike was not only the drummer but also the co-producer together with guitarist John Petrucci, as well as a significant contributing lyricist. Dream Theater is one of the most popular progressive rock bands in history and Mike Portnoy has been an integral part of this success. Other projects and artists that Portnoy has worked with over the years include Liquid Tension Experiment, Transatlantic, Neal Morse, Avenged Sevenfold and G3. Portnoy has also formed many tribute bands (Beatles, Led Zeppelin, The Who) to allow him to play some of his favourite music.

Portnoy has always been enthusiastic about education and he has released three full length tuition DVDs as well as books that demonstrate his approach to drumming, and in particular drumming in odd time signatures. In 2000 Portnoy won global awards for his educational work and since then has been one of the most inspiring educators in this style of drumming.

During 25 years with Dream Theater and his many side projects, Portnoy used very large and creative setups. One of his setups, named Mirage Monster, included six octobans, three bass drums, eight toms, a gong drum, over 25 cymbals and a gong. Portnoy has worked closely with drum manufacturer Tama and cymbal manufacturer Sabian since the eighties and developed two signature snare drums as well as three cymbal stacks known as Max Stax (named after his son). He also has his own signature sticks by Promark (model 420, a reference to Portnoy's birthday).

Recommended Listening

'6:00'
'The Dance of Eternity'
'On The Back Of Angels'

Steve Gadd

Steve Gadd is one of the best known and highly regarded session and studio drummers in the industry. His iconic drumming on tracks such as 'Aja', 'Fifty Ways to Leave Your Lover' and 'Late in the Evening' became classics that every drummer in the world will

study during their development. Gadd is known for always playing exactly what is needed and providing amazing groove regardless of the style. After using Gadd on one of his albums in the seventies, the great Chick Corea said, "Every drummer wants to play like Gadd because he plays perfect."

It is simply impossible to list every artist that Gadd has worked with but the most notable collaborations are: Simon and Garfunkel, Steely Dan, James Taylor, Eric Clapton, Chick Corea, Al Di Meola and Frank Sinatra. Gadd also recorded a dozen albums with his own projects as well as educational DVDs and many clinics and performances at international drum festivals. Gadd has worked with Yamaha drums and Zildjian cymbals since the eighties. Together with Zildjian he developed the Session cymbal range and he usually uses a few crashes, a ride and hi-hats from this range for every gig. Gadd's famous Yamaha kit consists of a 22" bass drum, 14" snare drum, two toms and two floor toms. With a few minor changes, this has essentially been Gadd's setup in every live and studio situation.

Gadd has won numerous international awards during his career, including an honorary Doctor of Music degree from Berklee College of Music for his outstanding contribution to contemporary music. However, most of all he won the respect and admiration of the whole drumming community worldwide because of his amazing musicianship and down-to-earth attitude.

Recommended Listening

'Aja'
'Fifty Ways To Leave Your Lover'
'Late In The Evening'

David Garibaldi

David Garibaldi started his professional career at the age of 17, and was soon working with artists such as Patti Austin, Natalie Cole, Yellowjackets, Larry Carlton and most notably the well known funk band Tower Of Power which he joined in 1970.

Tower Of Power have been performing since 1968 and together released over 25 albums, constantly touring worldwide and inspiring musicians to pursue their passion for funk and RnB music with a large horn section. Their biggest hits include 'What is Hip?', 'You're Still a Young Man', 'Soul with a Capital S', 'Funk the Dumb Stuff' and 'Soul Vaccination'. The sound of Tower Of Power's five-piece horn section became so popular that many artists hired them as session players, including Santana, Grateful Dead, Elton John, Aerosmith and Rod Stewart. The song 'So Very Hard To Go' was featured in the soundtrack of the film *City Of God* (2002) as well as *Semi-Pro* in 2008.

Garibaldi uses a standard six-piece Yamaha kit and a selection of Sabian cymbals. The most unique part of his set up is the additional 10" snare drum which is set to the left of the hi-hat. Garibaldi's book The Code of Funk has become a bible for funk drumming over the years and his unique funk grooves still inspire generations of young drummers all across the world.

Recommended Listening

'Diggin' on James Brown'
'What is Hip?'
'Pocketful of Soul'

Style Focus: Funk

Funk Rim Shot and Ghost Notes

One of the most important aspects of funk drumming is the use of many ghost notes and funk rim shots on the backbeats. Ghost notes have been covered previously, but you will see that coordinating these with advanced funk grooves can be challenging, especially if you strive to keep the dynamic level soft and controlled. The funk rim shot is generally higher in pitch than the usual rim shot and can be created by using a smaller snare drum or tuning your current snare to a higher pitch – but this will only be effective in the studio where you have time to adjust to the desired sound.

In live situations you can create this sound by pulling your hand backwards so the tip of the stick is about halfway between the rim and the centre of the drum. In this position, practise hitting the snare and surrounding rim at the same time. Listen to the sound and adjust if necessary. When you feel comfortable with this technique try **Ex. 1** below, and do not forget about the ghost notes. Remember, stylistic sound adjustments are not usually reflected in notation, but you should know when to switch according to the musical context.

1

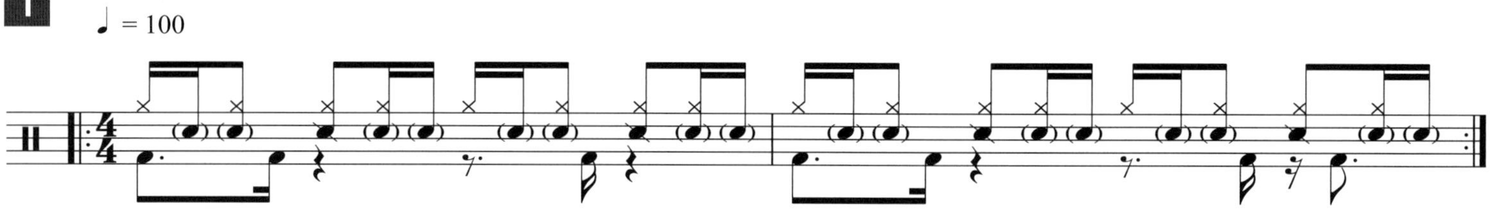

Open Hi-Hat Length

Another important feature of this style is the variety of length of the open hi-hats.

In **Ex. 2** you will see two open hi-hats: one as an eighth note and the other as a sixteenth note.

2

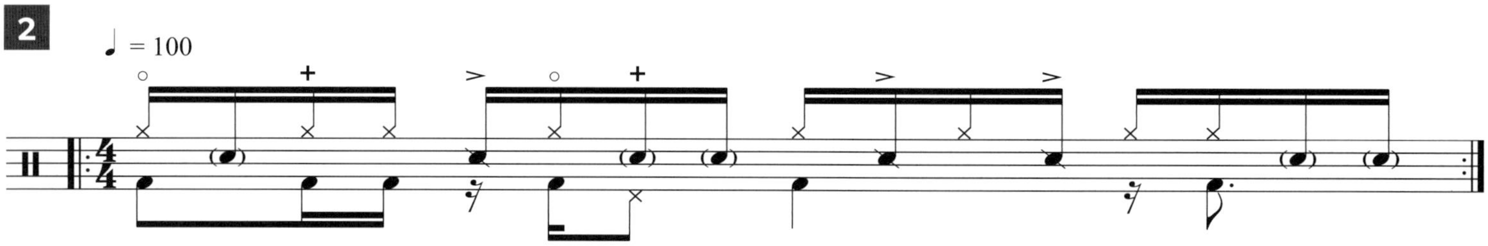

Second Hi-Hat

Many funk drummers choose to have an additional hi-hat in their setup. This is generally different in sound from the main hi-hat. It can use smaller cymbals, larger cymbals or even just be half open throughout. This is usually set on the right side, close to the ride cymbal. If you do not have another hi-hat in your setup, try using the ride cymbal as shown in **Ex. 3**. If you do, play all the ride cymbal strokes on your additional hi-hat. This concept will open your mind to the endless possibilities of grooves.

3

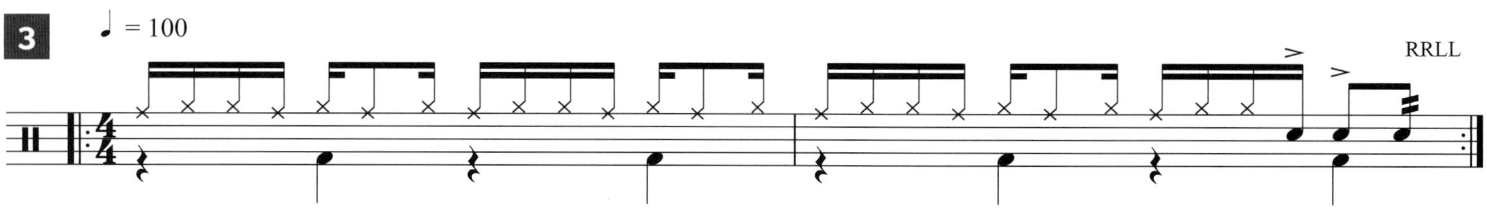

32nd notes

In mid tempo funk it is very common to embellish the groove with some 32nd notes, generally using the closed hi-hat. Although phrases of this type can be played with single strokes, you may find it easier to use double strokes. Ensure that the doubles are soft and controlled. Here is an example with this concept:

4

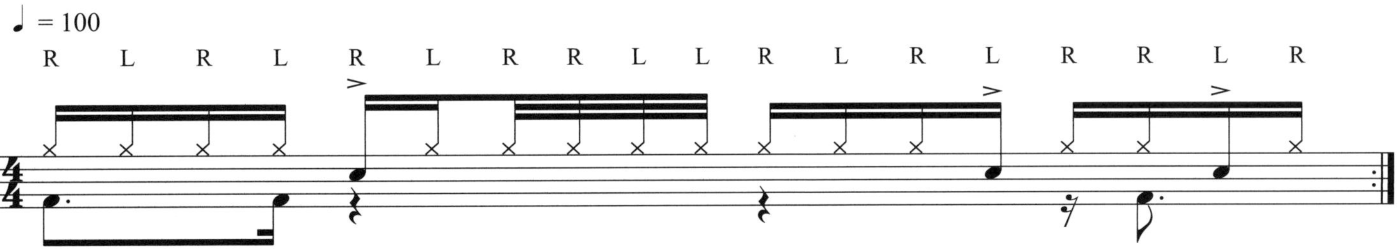

Linear Funk

In this funk groove the hands will be using the linear concept. This means that drum voices played with the hands will not be played together in this groove. Keep your right hand on the hi-hat and play the snare with the left hand. The sticking combines the standard and inverted paradiddles. Check out Garibaldi, Mike Clark and Rick Latham for more linear funk inspiration.

5

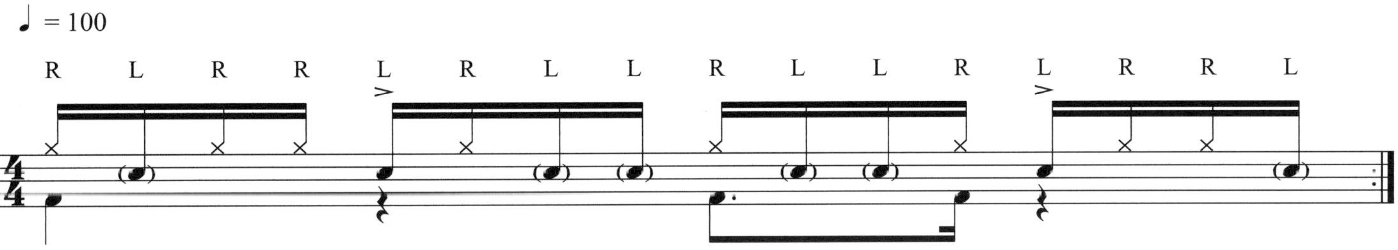

In **Ex. 6** and **7** we will explore this concept when used in the time signature of 12/8. Focus on the sticking and snare sounds until you achieve a solid groove. In **Ex. 7** you will see one possible variation of the same groove, where the hi-hat pattern is played on the bell of the ride cymbal. If you have a cowbell in your set up, try playing the hi-hat pattern on it. This is a variation used by many funk drummers including Garibaldi.

6

7

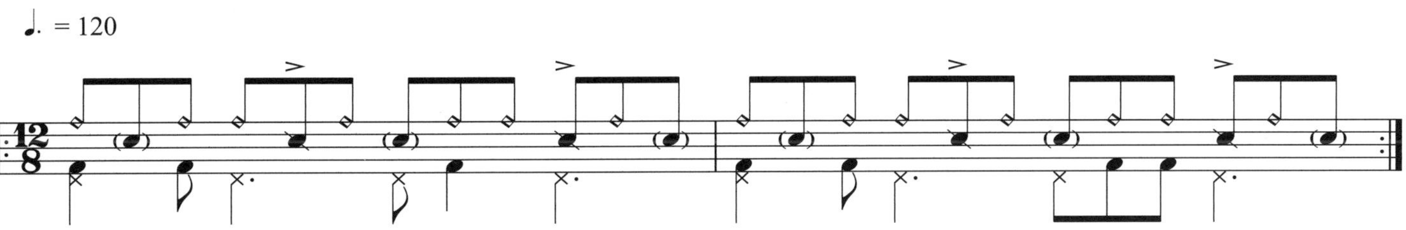

Piece Preparation: 'Oakland Vibe'

This piece is in the funk style of David Garibaldi, Clyde Stubblefield and Zigaboo Modeliste. The backing track of 'Oakland Vibe' can be downloaded for free from **www.vvinner.com/downloads**.

A Intro

This section has a stylistic funk breakdown pattern played between the hi-hat and ride cymbal. If you have a second hi-hat in your setup, the pattern will also be very effective using right and left hi-hats. If you follow the notation you will see that the sticking suggested in **Ex. 1** makes most sense. However, you should always feel free to adapt according to your setup and technique.

B Verse

In the verse we have a funk beat using the hi-hat, snare and bass drum. The snare has two main sounds: rim shot and ghost notes. These two sounds are integral in funk (see p. 30 for more detail on this). Start your practice with the hi-hat playing consistent eighth notes throughout as notated in **Ex. 2**. When you feel comfortable with this groove add the notated hi-hat pattern that includes eighth notes and sixteenth notes. Coordinating this hi-hat pattern with the snare and bass drum and achieving flow might take some practice. Remember many great funk drummers that you already know apply a touch of swing feel to this type of groove. Try to find your own signature funk swing feel while working on this performance piece. In the second part of the verse you are free to add groove variations which are suitable for the style.

C Chorus

The chorus groove focuses on the ride cymbal. The funky snare and bass drum pattern is different from the verse, mainly because the second snare in every group of four strokes is played an eighth note later than usual. This displacement gives the groove a unique flow which is very funky but must be played with a solid sense of time.

At this level it is important to remember and utilise the four different strokes that you have learned throughout this series (Full, Down, Up and Tap) as well as the Gladstone Technique concept. **Ex. 3** shows an example of this. Understanding and applying this concept to your playing will improve your sound and overall feel.

D Keyboard Solo

The main groove in this section follows a rhythmic leading pattern of one eighth note followed by two sixteenth notes. The notated voicing of open and closed hi-hat should be developed accordingly to your understanding of the style from bar 49.

The next stage will be to focus on the notated variations and fills, and combine them with the grooves that you have already practised. **Ex. 4** shows the suggested sticking for the sextuplet drum fill that ends this section.

E Drum Solo

In this section you have four bars to solo. Use all the tools that have been explored in this series as well as the stylistic understanding you have developed, and apply these in your solo. Most importantly, ensure that the pulse is secure and you are constructing phrases that make musical sense, as opposed to just playing a series of your fastest rudiments. Practising soloing with a metronome for about 10 minutes a day will help you develop a repertoire of improvised phrases, which will essentially become part of your sound. Writing down these ideas will help you constantly improve your soloing ability.

F Outro

After your drum solo you will reach the final section of the piece. This is in the time signature of $\frac{5}{4}$, and we have an interesting funk interpretation rather than a classic $\frac{4}{4}$ groove. The suggested sticking patterns for the two grooves in this section are detailed in **Ex. 5** & **6**. The alternate sticking in **Ex. 5** follows an important stylistic ethos used often by funk drummer Zigaboo Modeliste. Other areas to focus on in this section: the lengths of the open hi-hat, the challenging fill in bar 67 and the syncopated hits in the final bar.

The last four bars of this section include a development of the previous groove. Although you can keep playing with the same sticking, the suggested sticking in **Ex. 6** will help you achieve the ghost note consistency with ease. Finally, ensure that you can play the final fill very well in order to achieve a convincing ending.

1
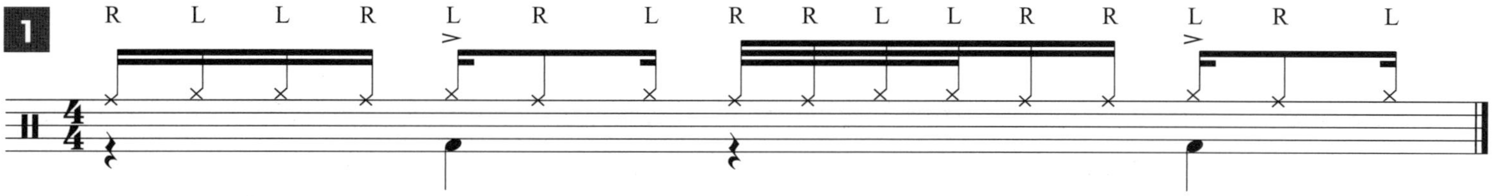

2

3
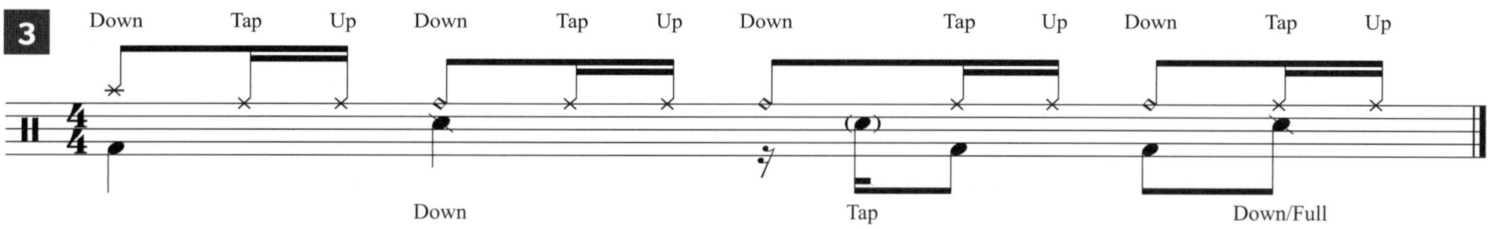

4
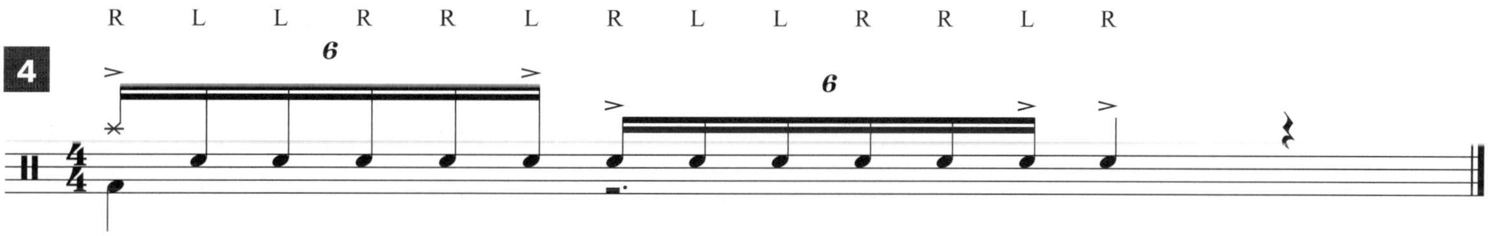

5
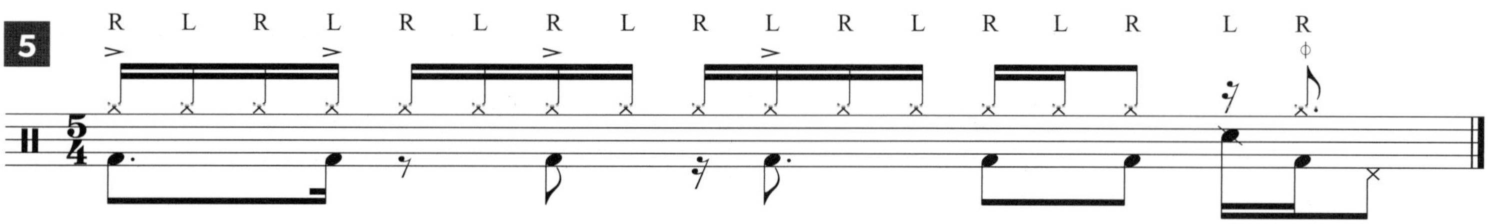

6
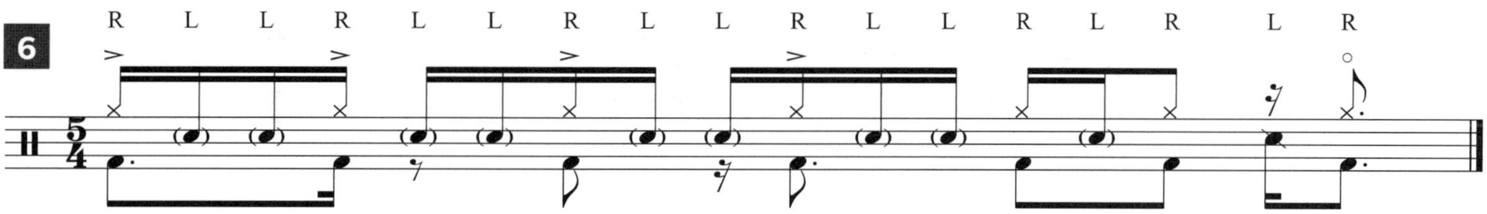

'Oakland Vibe'

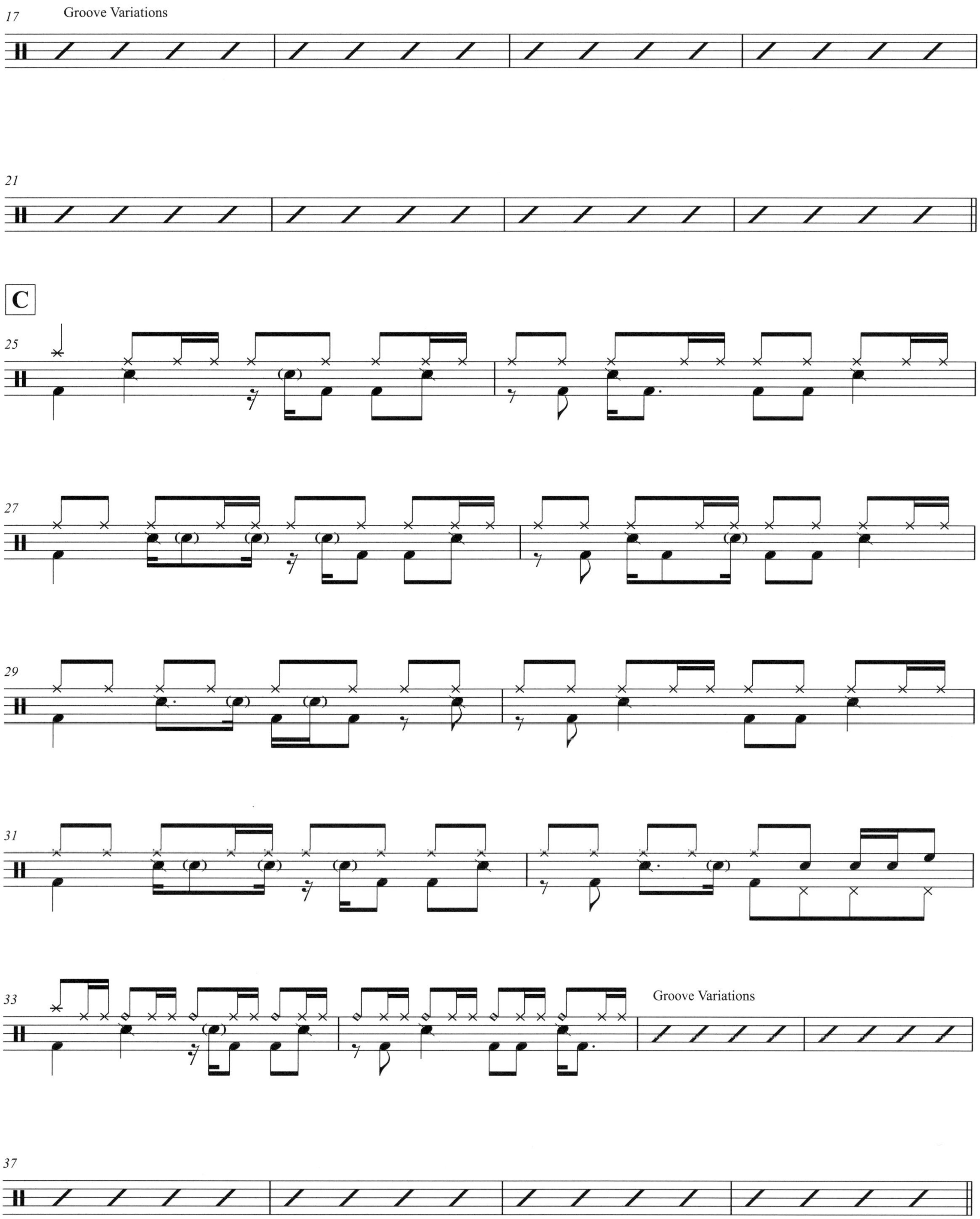
17
Groove Variations
21
C
25
27
29
31
33
Groove Variations
37

D
41
43
45
47
49
Develop (7 bars)
51
53
55
6
6

E
Drum solo (4 bars)
57
F
61
63
65
67

Moeller Technique and Rudiments

Moeller Technique

Named after the drummer Sanford Moeller, this technique is based on a whipping motion, producing fast strokes with minimum effort.

First of all, let's focus on the whipping motion. Start by lifting your arm and allowing your wrist to drop. Then, in one smooth motion, drop your arm and allow the wrist to accept the whipping force created by the motion. This should lead to a solid accented stroke. Practise with both hands at a slow tempo, keeping your body balanced and relaxed. Allow the fingers around the stick to move freely without losing control of the stick. When this is done correctly it feels like bouncing a ball.

Having mastered and internalised this whipping motion, it is time to discuss the rebound. The classic Moeller stroke is a series of three strokes on each hand where the first stroke is accented. Most drummers agree that the strokes that follow the accent are the natural rebound of the whip motion.

If this is done correctly, any drummer will be able to double or even triple their speed of playing without risk of injury.

Obviously, the Moeller stroke can be applied to phrases with one rebound (**Ex. 2**), three rebounds (**Ex. 3**) and even more. However, most phrases will use combinations of the three exercises shown below.

Drummers that do not agree with the rebound concept claim that each stroke must actually be played. What they actually mean by that is when playing at slow tempos the whipping motion of the Moeller technique can be integrated with controlled rebounds from the Gladstone Technique. However, when attempting fast tempos, the rebound Moeller must come into affect.

This is only the tip of the iceberg and I recommend that you continue to study this advanced technique with a teacher, and check out drummers and educators such as Jim Chapin, Joe Morello and Dom Famularo.

1

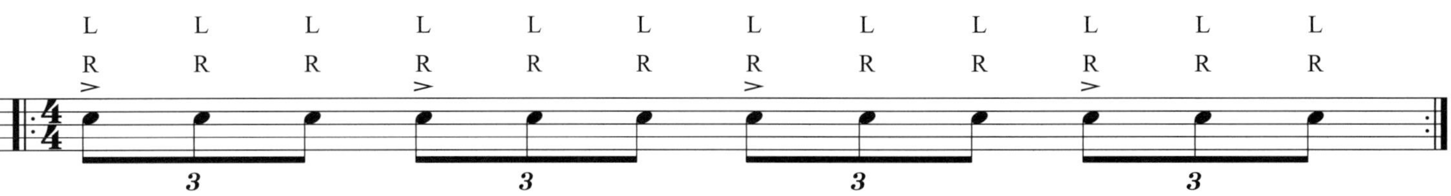

2

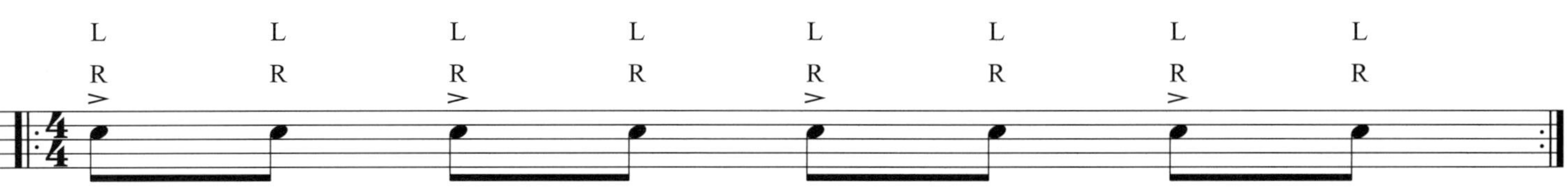

3

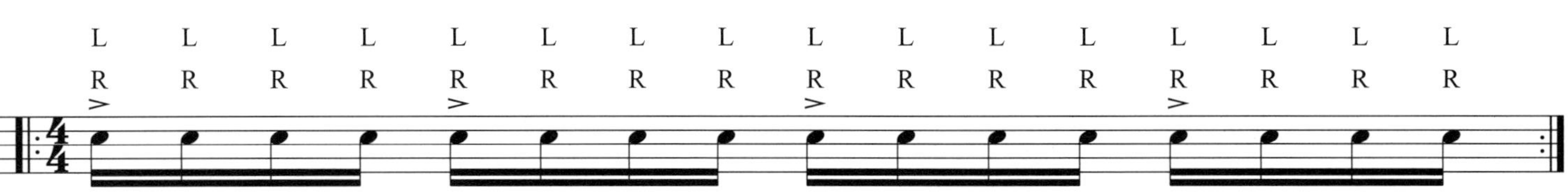

Rudiments

Double Ratamacue

This rudiment is similar to the single ratamacue, with an added eighth note drag on each side to make it three quarter notes in total. Aim to use the concept of the Moeller technique as well as the Gladstone technique. Incorporating these techniques into your playing effectively will lead to greater control. As always feel free to focus on right hand lead first, then on the left, and then put it all together.

1

Pataflafla

The Pataflafla is one of the best rudiments for strengthening your wrists and stick control. It is notated in sixteenth notes, with accented flams on the first and last sixteenth note of each beat. Make sure you also practise this rudiment starting with your following hand.

2

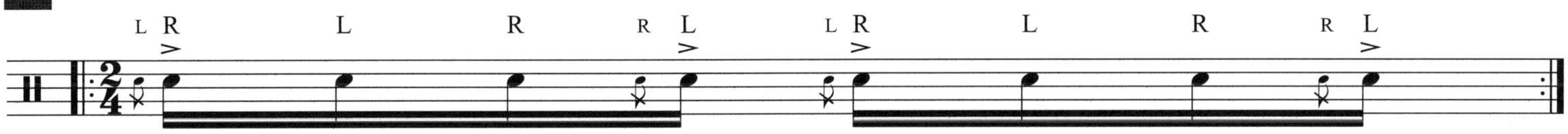

Hybrid Paradiddle

This hybrid rudiment combines a paradiddle-diddle and a single paradiddle into one rhythmic phrase that flows from right hand lead to left hand lead. Once you have mastered this phrase try voicing it in a musical way around the kit.

3

Advanced Double Bass Drum

Consistent patterns

In this lesson you will find a selection of the most important double bass drum patterns. Practise these at various tempos and ensure that you can move between them smoothly. Your right foot will obviously be stronger at this point, especially if you have worked on the advanced techniques discussed on p. 8–9.

Now it is time to strengthen your left foot and focus on the balance and the sound projection of both bass drum beaters. If you need inspiration for double bass drum playing check out Louie Bellson, Keith Moon, Ginger baker, Billy Cobham, Dave Lombardo, Tomas Haake and Steve Smith.

1

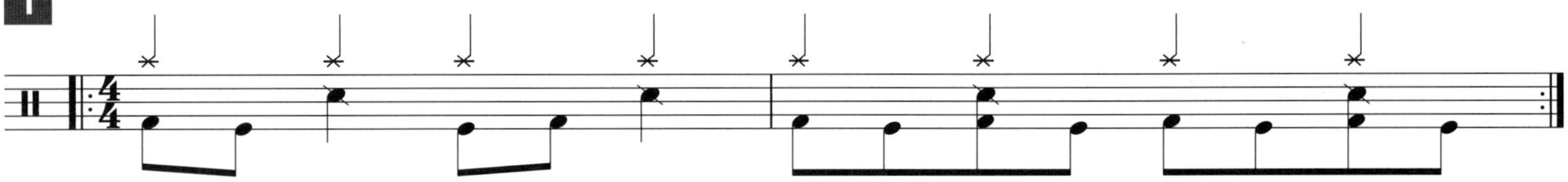

2

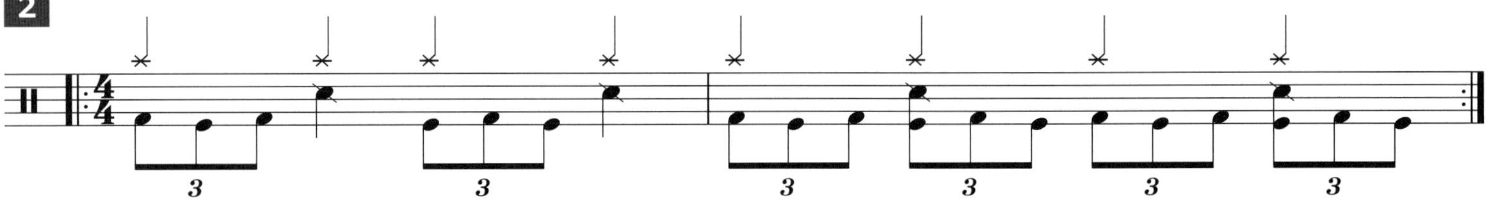

3

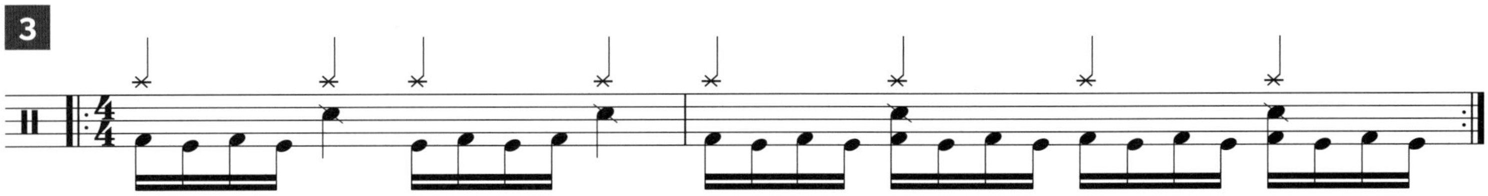

4

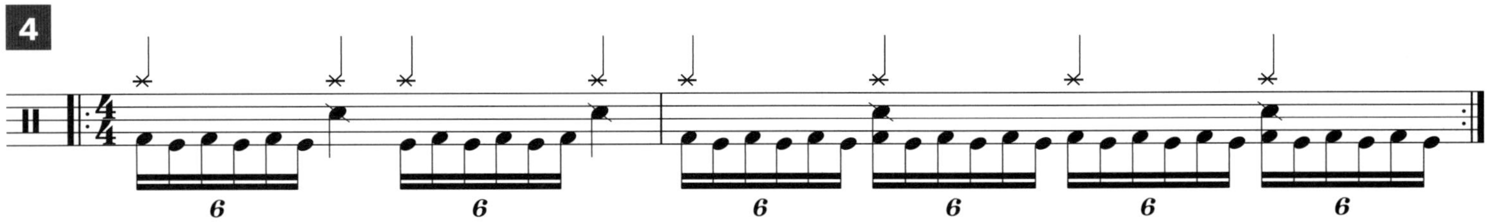

Tip!

Although most drummers lead their double bass drumming with their right foot, drummers such as Keith Moon and Gregg Bissonette are known for leading with their left. Experiment and see what works best for you.

Phrasing

Another advanced concept involves using the double bass drum as another facility to play rhythmic phrases around the kit. This can be used in a variety of styles and requires highly secure bass drum technique.

Remember to practise these grooves at various dynamic levels to ensure maximum control.

1 ♩ = 140

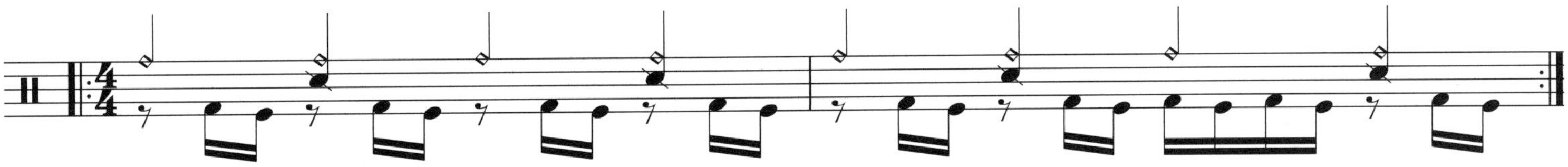

2 ♩ = 90

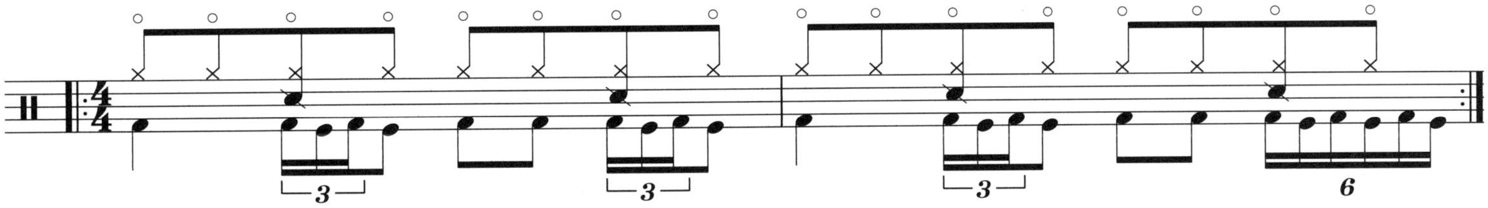

3 ♩ = 90

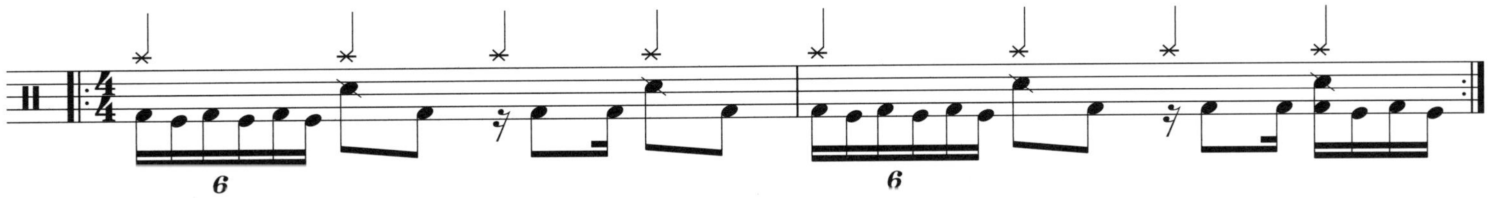

4 ♩ = 90

5 ♩ = 80

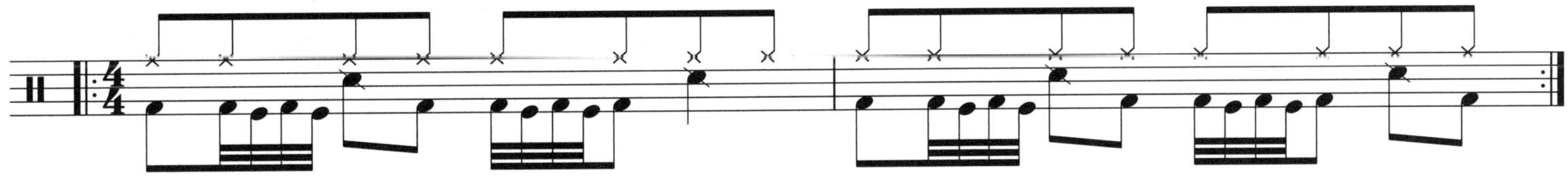

6 ♩ = 100

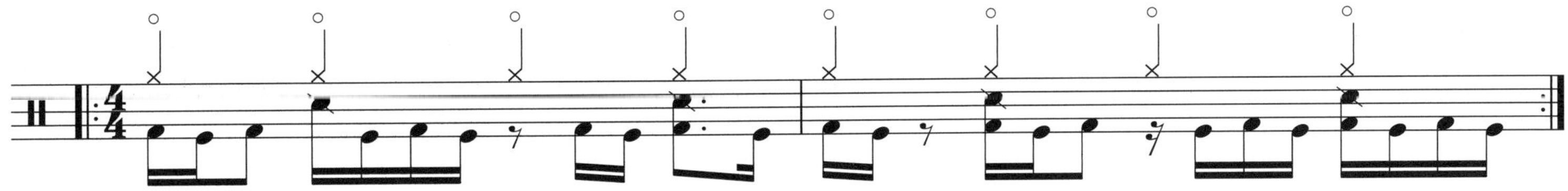

Rolls

Buzz Roll

The buzz roll technique was explained earlier in this series (Level 1, p. 51). In this lesson we will show you how to incorporate it into your drumming. When performing a continuous buzz roll (also known as a multiple-bounce roll) it is important to produce a smooth sound and have the ability to play it at all dynamic levels.

However, it is equally important to use secure stick control in order to play short one-handed buzz rolls within phrases. The exercises below will explore this concept. Feel free to develop these and create individual variations as well as moving around the kit.

1

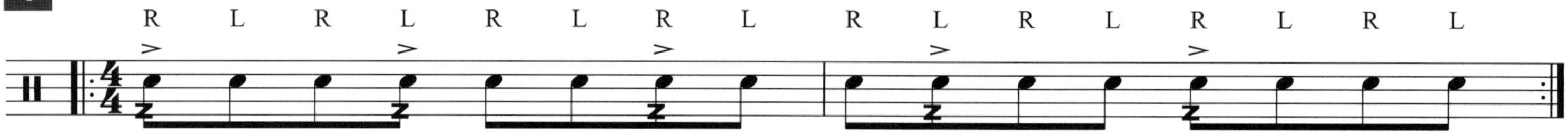

2

3

4

5

Combined Rolls

The combined roll exercises below use five, seven and nine stroke rolls. Practise the rhythms first and ensure that you are fully aware which sticking to use for each roll, then combine the rolls.

Start at a slow tempo and aim for accurate and defined phrases. Finally, increase the speed and experiment with moving parts of the phrases around the kit.

1

2

3

Now let's add the buzz rolls as well. Choose and adapt the sticking to fit your technique.

4

5

Polyrhythms

Polyrhythms are defined as multiple rhythms (two or more) that are played at the same time.

Generally, polyrhythms are challenging but exciting to play. To internalise a polyrhythm we need to be able to 'hear' both rhythms at the same time. When practising a basic polyrhythm try saying or singing each rhythm.

Playing a systemic polyrhythm is also known as cross-rhythm in the drumming world.

Let's start with a polyrhythm of 2 over 3 (also known as 4 over 6). This can be written two ways (compare **1A** and **1B**).

1A

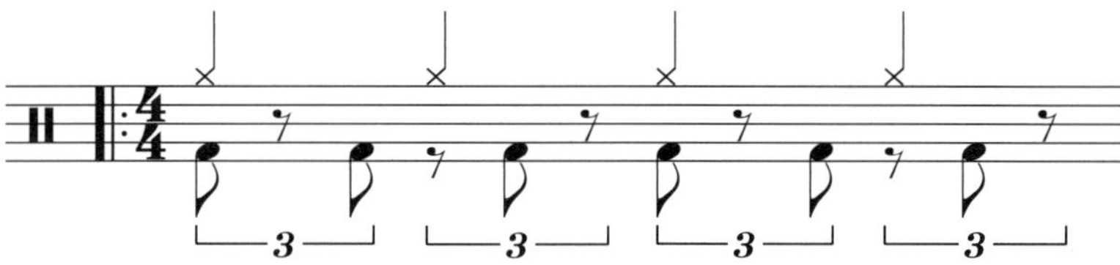

1B

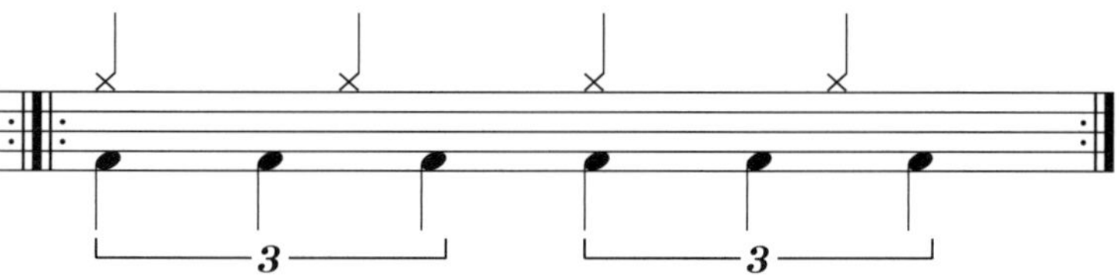

And here is the 2 over 3 polyrhythm in a shuffle interpretation.

2

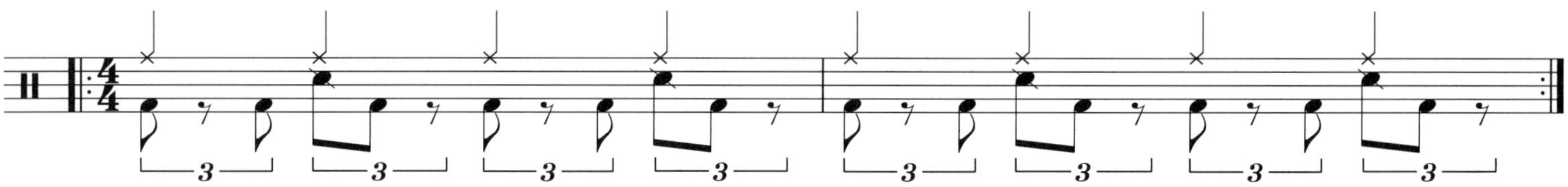

If we swap the parts around we get the 3 over 2 polyrhythm.

3A

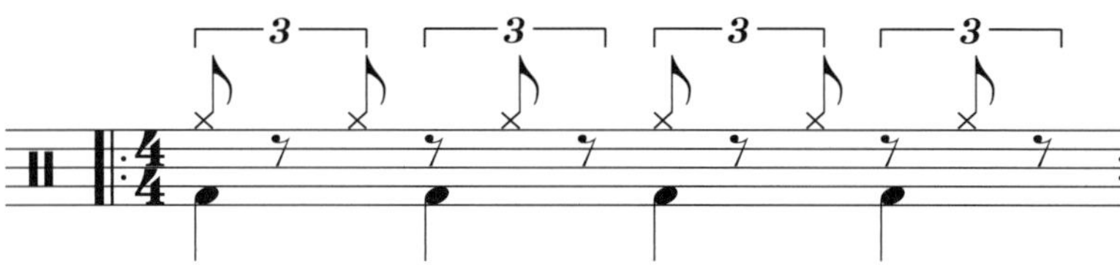

3B

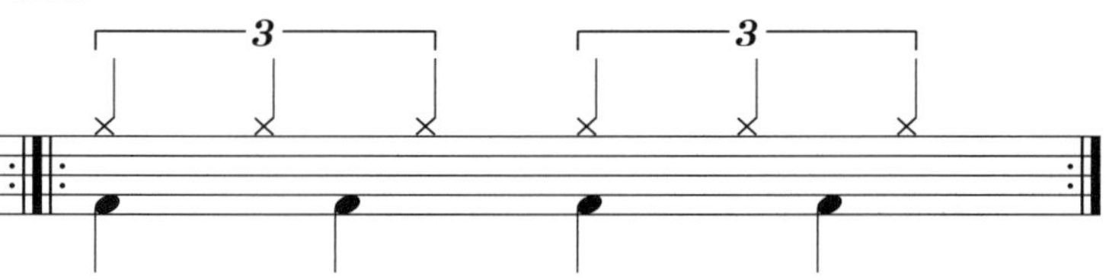

Ex. 4 is a modern hip hop interpretation of this polyrhythm. Play the sixteenth note hi-hat and backbeat snare with your left hand. The right hand plays the first and third strokes of each set of triplets on the hi-hat.

If you are interested in polyrhythms check out these drummers: Danny Carrey, Thomas Haake, Terry Bozzio, Gavin Harrison, Neil Peart, Bill Bruford and Chris 'Daddy' Dave.

4

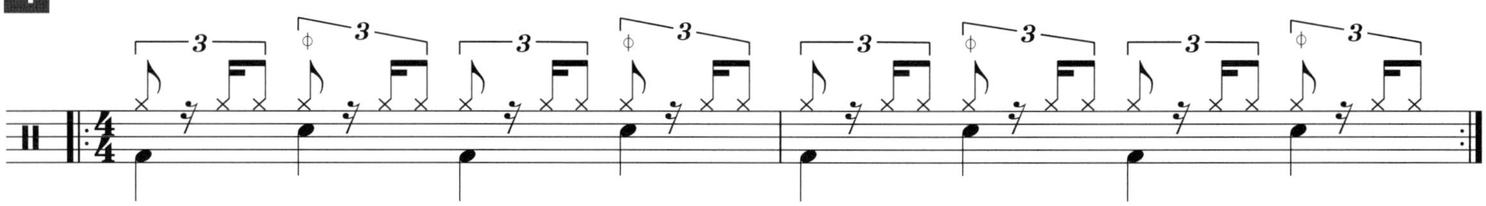

Now, let's look at a few more polyrhythms. This lesson should give you a basic idea of what is possible once you understand polyrhythms and will inspire you to continue and research this subject.

Remember that when learning a new polyrhythm you can practise it with your hands first in order to understand it. You can also use advanced metronome apps that allow you to hear any polyrhythm you wish.

1 3 Over 4 Polyrhythm

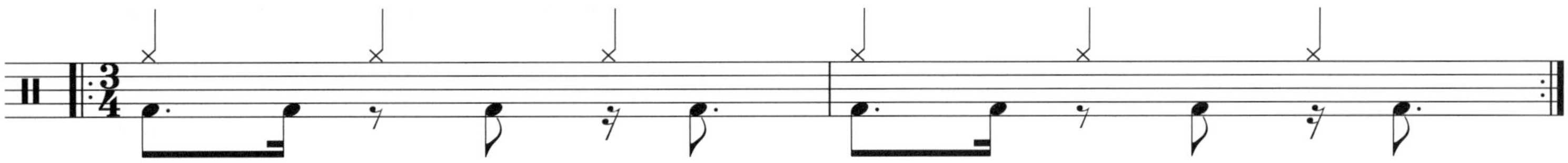

2 3 Over 4 Polyrhythm Groove

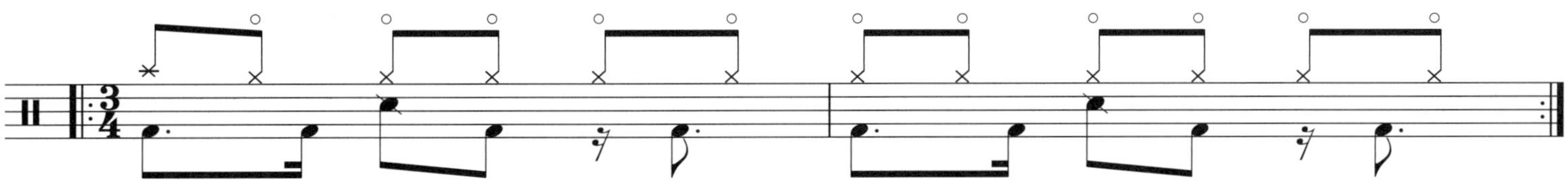

3 3 Over 4 Polyrhythm Phrase

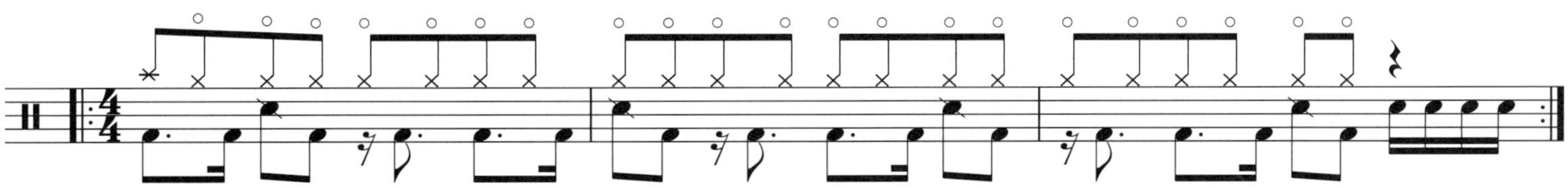

4 5 Over 4 Polyrhythm

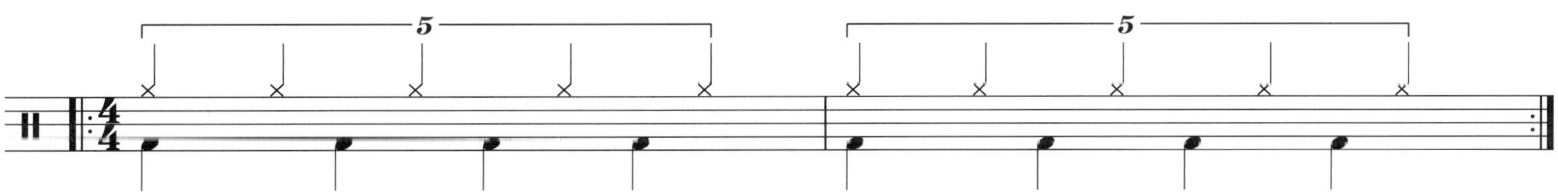

5 4 Over 5 Polyrhythm

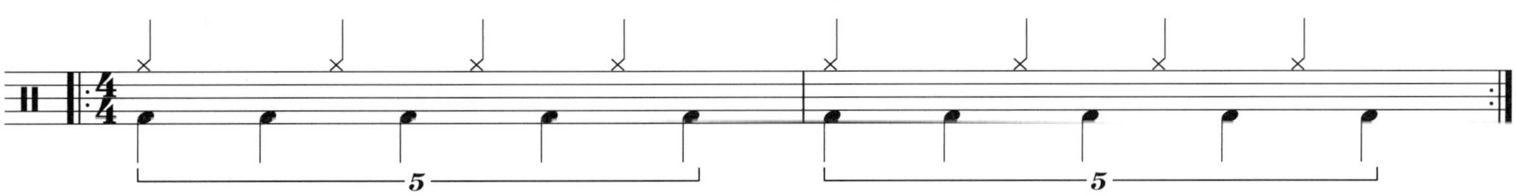

6 5 Over 4 Polyrhythm Groove

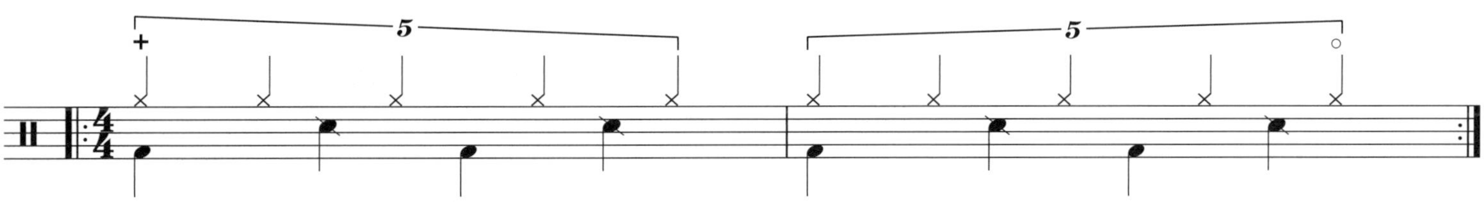

Drumming in Seven

This lesson explores grooves in seven, starting with grooves in 7/4 which means seven quarter notes per bar.

Practise these with a metronome or a musical loop in 7/4 to ensure that you are playing the exercises correctly. It will take time until you feel comfortable with this odd time signature so be patient. When confident try to add some 7/4 fills to these grooves.

Ex. 1–3 below demonstrate a few different approaches to grooves in 7/4 .

Ex. 4 is a fast tempo 7/4 groove which can be effective in many styles of music.

1 ♩ = 90

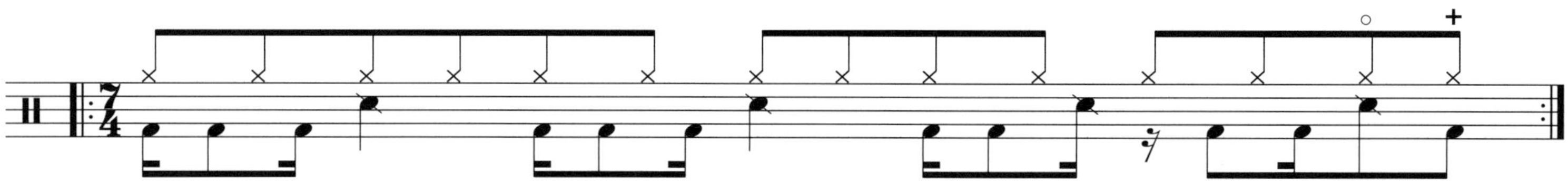

2 ♩ = 90

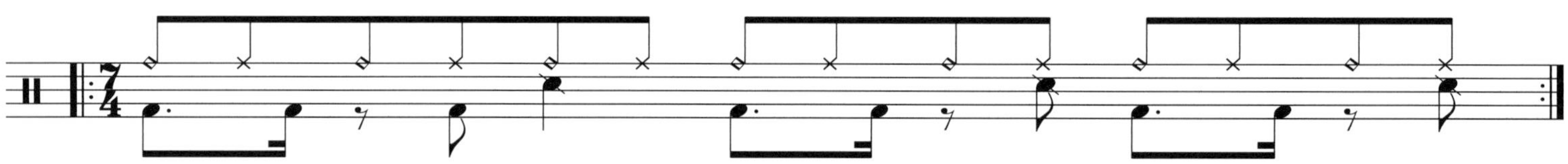

3 ♩ = 90

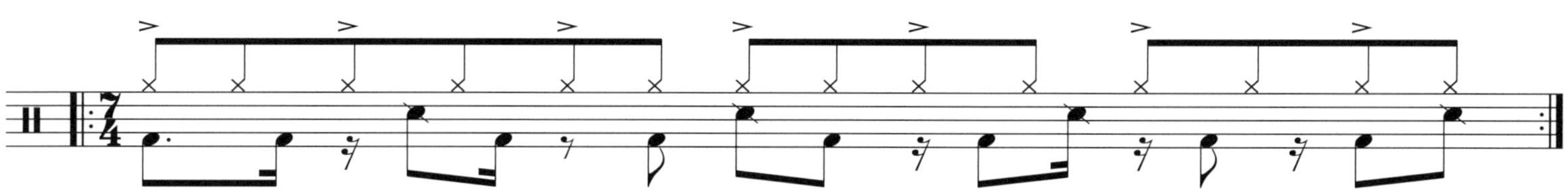

4 ♩ = 160

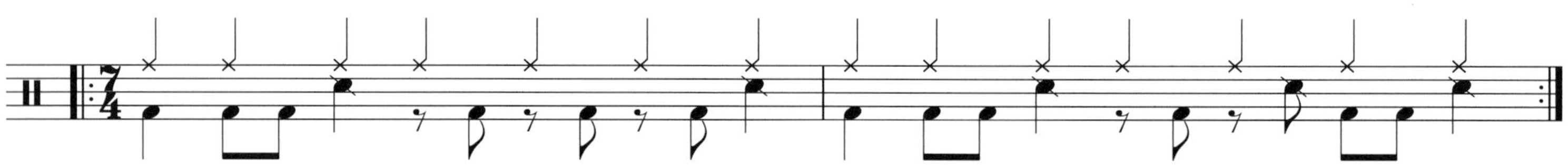

Now let's take a fast 7/4 groove and add one bar of 4/4 . This essentially creates a compound groove of 11/4 which can lead to creative patterns. If you play with a band that explores time signatures like these, try suggesting a groove similar to the one below and creating a composition that is based on your groove.

5 ♩ = 160

$\frac{7}{8}$ Grooves

Now let's look at some grooves in $\frac{7}{8}$. This means that we have seven eighth notes per bar.

The most common ways of counting seven eighths are 2+2+3 and 3+2+2. The speed and style will usually suggest the most suitable counting.

1 ♩ = 135

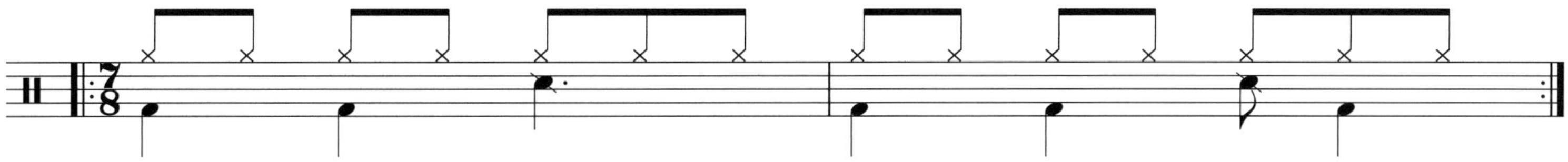

2 ♩ = 105

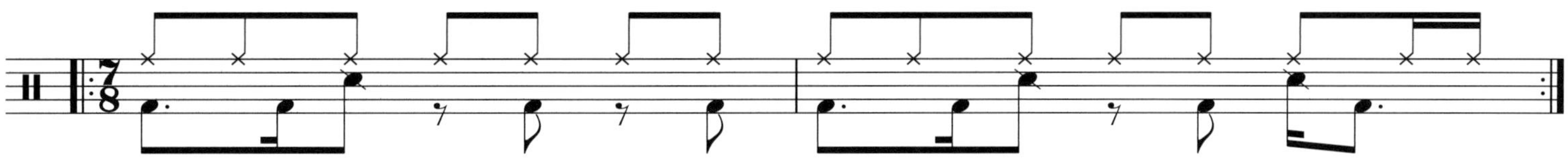

3 ♩ = 90

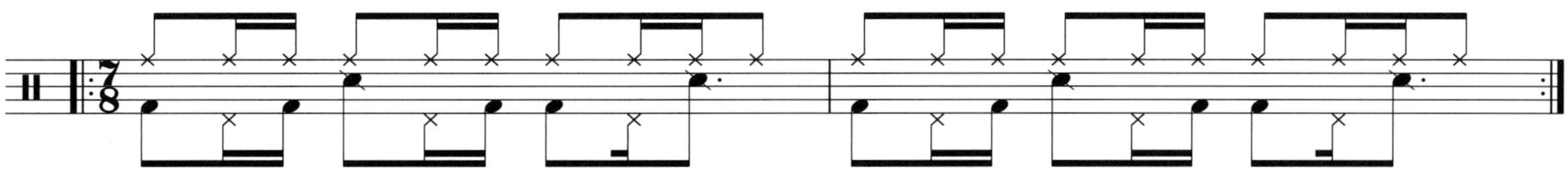

$\frac{7}{8}$ Grooves

Fills in seven can be challenging, especially if you are not completely sure where the '1' is. Take your time, practise slowly and adapt the fills to suit the time signature, your technical ability and your musical taste.

> **Tip!**
>
> *Check out these tracks in seven:*
> *Pink Floyd: 'Money' (predominantly in $\frac{7}{4}$)*
> *Rush: 'Tom Sawyer' (instrumental sections in $\frac{7}{8}$)*
> *Tool: 'Ticks and Leeches' ($\frac{7}{4}$)*

4 ♩ = 135

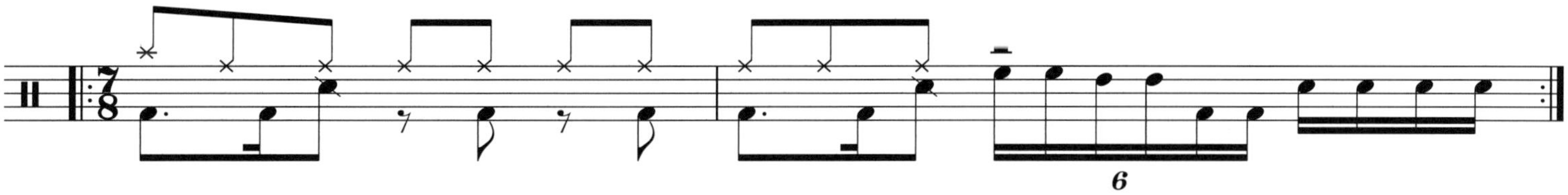

5 ♩ = 90

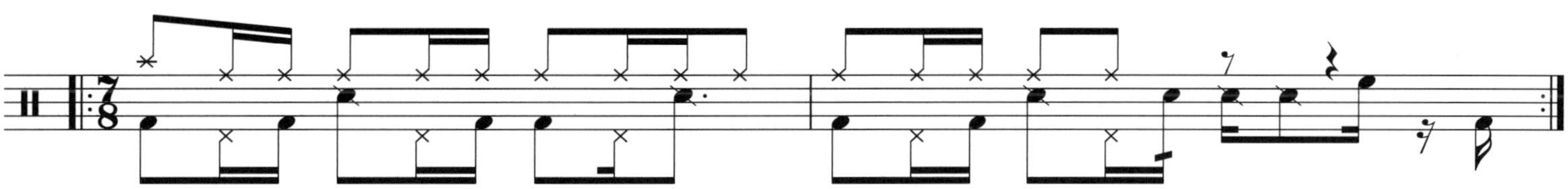

Gospel Chops

The term gospel chops has become popular as gospel drummers with immense technical ability have demonstrated to the world that church drumming can be very exciting. The exercises in this chapter will give you a glimpse into some of the concepts used when playing gospel fills. Each concept is limitless so once you understand it try experimenting with different rhythms, voicings and practise at various speeds. Finally try adding accents and dynamics for greater musical shape.

The foundation of many gospel fills (chops) is combining rhythmic phrases which vary in length in an unorthodox way. These phrases are usually created from groups of 2 and 3.

The three exercises below explore variations of 2:2 phrases. Practise them until you feel confident and then move on to **Ex. 4**.

1

2

3

Now, let's mix them together to create a more interesting phrase.

4

To create more musical shape, you can choose to add accents and dynamics.

5

Let's try a more adventurous grouping next – 3:1:3:2. This is a classic grouping in gospel drumming and it will also be very effective when played in triplets.

1

Another common grouping in gospel drumming is 5:5:5:1. This will be effective in sixteenth notes (as notated) and also in thirty-second notes.

2

Here is an example of how to incorporate the standard paradiddle rudiment and create a ten-note phrase.

3

Ex. 4 uses two other rudiments to create a convincing gospel fill: the pataflafla and the Swiss army triplet. The Swiss army triplet will be discussed in detail in P.69 of this book.

Practise this slowly at first to understand which sticking patterns are being used, then implement the voicings and increase the speed.

4

This gospel fill offers another creative use of groupings and sticking.

5

New Orleans Style

The modern New Orleans drumming style (also known as second line or street beat) has developed from the drum and percussion patterns played by brass marching bands in the late 1800s and more traditional African music of the early 1800s. The grooves as adapted for the drum kit have a unique and uplifting feel. New Orleans drumming is based on two Afro-Haitian rhythms: the Tresillo and Cinquilolo. The rhythmic foundation of both of these (also known as the clave) is notated in **Ex. 1–2** below.

In **Ex. 3–4** we will voice these rhythms on the snare drum with the modern feet pattern approach of Second Line. Notice the buzz rolls in **Ex. 5**: this is a very important sound in New Orleans drumming. Initially, add the buzz rolls and accents as notated in **Ex. 5**, then try moving the buzz rolls to different notes and find convincing and musical combinations.

1

2

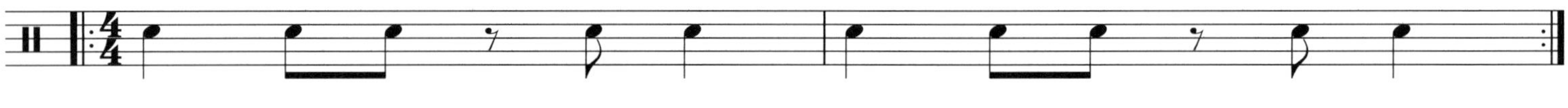

3

4

5

Playing Between the Cracks

The most important element of New Orleans drumming is the concept of playing with a slightly swung feel. This also commonly referred to as 'playing between the cracks'. This is not usually notated but is crucial for grooves of this type to sound convincing.

Practise **Ex. 1** repeatedly in the following way: the first play all strokes completely straight, the second time completely swung and the third time slightly swung, (between the two). Once you feel comfortable, apply this to the grooves on the previous page.

1 ♩ = 175

Stylistic Sticking

Until now you have probably been playing these grooves with alternate sticking. This is absolutely fine and can be very convincing as long as the feel is right. However, New Orleans drummers often use stylistic sticking that actually follows the accented strokes. With this concept it is straightforward to vary the voicing of the groove and orchestrate it differently around the kit.

2 ♩ = 175

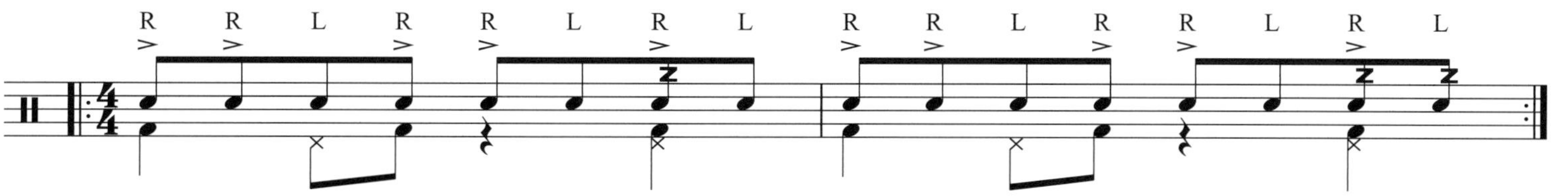

Here is a variation with the right hand leading on the ride cymbal. This leading pattern can also be very effective on the bell of ride, cowbell, woodblock, rim or shell of any of the drums.

3 ♩ = 175

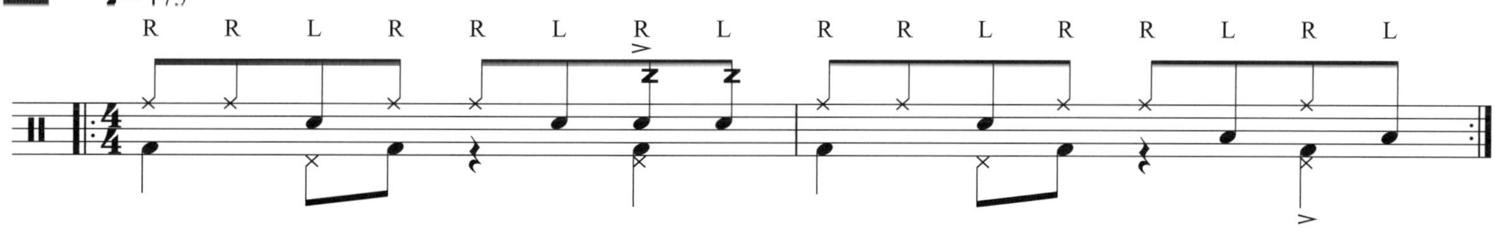

Another stylistic sound used often by Second Line drummers is the jingle stick as it is clearly emulates the tambourine sound which is fundamental in New Orleans music.

In the next groove the right hand plays the floor tom with a jingle stick and the left hand plays the snare. Adjust your snare wires to the off position to achieve more authentic and traditional sound.

4

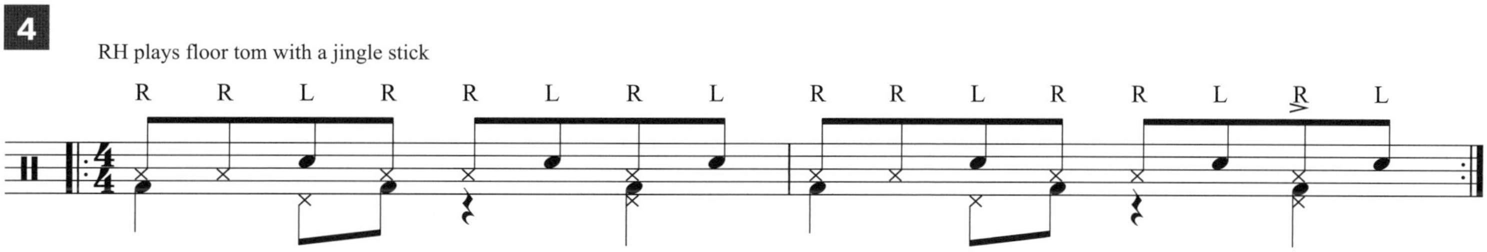

Musicianship

Recording

In this lesson we will focus on another crucial element of being a professional musician: recording.

If you have already started gigging and made contacts in the industry some people might ask you to record drums for them. This is probably because you can play solid grooves with good sound. Recording is another way to produce income from playing your instrument, and although this market is very competitive, it can also be very lucrative.

Building on the fundamentals presented in *Playing Live* (p. 22), let's look at some additional requirements for being a successful session drummer.

Get Comfortable with the Click

The ability to either play with a click effortlessly or provide a consistent pulse without one is very important for session work. Nowadays most session work is done with a click as this enables the producer to edit, add and change elements at any stage of the production. If you have followed this series, you should be very comfortable playing with a click. However, if you feel that this element needs strengthening do not wait and plan a way to improve this essential skill.

Get the Details

Once you have been booked for the session find out as much as possible about it including the length of the session, what type of music you will be playing and whether you will have to read or improvise your part. Try to find out about the artist, the producer, the studio, what equipment you are expected to bring and any other relevant information.

Get the Right Gear

With all of the above questions answered, think about the equipment (gear) you want to take. Apart from having all the essentials, ensure that the drums are tuned and ready to go. You may not have time to spare and studio time is expensive.

Recording in a studio is a creative process so make sure you have some options to offer the artist and/or producer during the session. Many drummers tend to take more than one snare drum and a variety of cymbals to a recording session. You might also want to bring any percussion instruments that you feel comfortable playing and any part of your gear that makes you and your sound unique.

Ensure that you have everything that you might need for the session, as not having anything essential will make you look unprofessional.

Get Techy

Generally, every recording session will have an artist, producer and at least one recording engineer. In smaller sessions, you might only have one additional person that does it all. It will be highly beneficial for you to become familiar with the essentials of drum recording. This is merely for you to be able to offer a better service and not advise the recording engineer or the producer how to do their jobs.

Aim to read about the basics of drum recording. If you are able, buy your own microphone set and experiment with home recordings until you achieve the best results from your drum kit. Alternatively, you can gain knowledge and experiment with different equipment if you get a job (even unpaid) in any recording studio or academic institution that has these facilities. Ensure that you listen back to the recordings, make notes about how you can improve and implement changes in your next recording practice. This knowledge and experience will put you in a much better position than a drummer who lacks this understanding.

Once you feel confident with your recording skills you can also offer another service which is known as a remote session.

Remote Sessions

These have become much more popular during the past decade due to the evolution of technology. This could be another stream of income for you as a professional musician. Remote sessions are generally booked online. You provide the client with your recordings in the agreed format and once they are pleased with your work you get paid. Offering remote drum recording sessions involves having a studio or space you can hire to record yourself, a good set of microphones, and someone (ideally yourself) with the knowledge and expertise to get a convincing sound from the drums.

Remember that once you have all these, you need to promote yourself (in person and online) with this specific purpose. Be knowledgeable about your recording equipment, mixing desk, microphones etc. and share this with your future clients. In addition, make sure that you have an updated credit list of artists you worked with and promote any audio/video files of you recording in the studio.

Ask the Experts

There is no better way of finding your path than by asking the experts and leaders in your field. In today's technologically advanced and connected world we are all able to access vast amounts of information and potentially make contact with anyone in our profession. Many of the experts in any field offer online lessons and support. If you are finding it hard to reach anyone specific, look at some of their existing materials (recordings, interviews, live shows, blogs, social media) in order to understand how they became so successful. This is such a valuable tool, so if you are serious about pursuing music as a career, I urge you to explore this further.

Feedback

It is important to ask for feedback, be open and take onboard any criticism from your clients and other players. This is especially important when starting to build your reputation, as acting on advice will help you improve your service. Once your client is happy with the result, ask for a positive testimonial for your website. This will help to convince new clients that you know what you are doing.

Be Patient, Enjoy the Ride

The career of a session drummer is one of the most sought after jobs on the planet, not only because the money can be good and you may even get paid more via royalty payments in years to come, but because it is a highly rewarding and creative process.

You can not expect this to happen immediately – you can only hope that when the phone call you have been waiting for all your life finally arrives you are prepared to take the opportunity.

Be patient and work with ambition, enthusiasm and full commitment. Even though it may take years to reach your goal, why not take the time to look around you, smile, appreciate the view and enjoy the ride?

Playing In The Pocket

This is probably the most advanced and important aspect of drum recording. Playing in the pocket refers to playing with a solid sense of pulse, the appropriate stylistic feel and awareness to everything else that is played by the other musicians. This crucial aspect of your drumming will develop in time as long as you understand the concepts and use your most valuable tool: your ears.

Your listening abilities will determine how far you can progress as a musician. Therefore, ensure that on a daily basis you listen to music. I do not mean listen to music while you do something else but actually sitting down, focused and listening to something specific that you choose in order to help you progress. Make notes while you are listening and create additional practice concepts that can be added to your practice log. Research the artists you listen to and aim to understand their concepts thoroughly. This process will sharpen your ears and make you more sensitive when playing with other musicians.

Playing in the pocket is sometimes referred to as playing slightly behind and in front of the beat. This is an important concept for you to explore, especially when playing styles of music such as funk and hip hop. However, be sensitive and do not use this where inappropriate. For example, if you are recording a pop album and playing everything with a 'lazy' feel (behind the beat), the producer might think that you are actually not a very good drummer and will not use you again.

Melodic Soloing

Pitch

In order to start exploring melodic soloing we need to understand the concept of pitch and how this can be translated on to the drum kit. If you have played a melodic instrument (piano, guitar, trumpet etc.) you will know that all instruments follow notation which not only signifies rhythms but also pitch. The pitches are the exact notes that should be played according to the notation. Pitches and rhythms are used together to create melodies.

The drum kit is mainly a rhythmic instrument and many drummers choose to focus on the rhythmic aspect when soloing. However, the concept of melodic soloing can add a whole new dimension to your solos. With practice you will be able to play simple melodies on the drum kit by the end of this lesson.

Tuning

Drummers such as Terry Bozzio and Neil Peart have taken the melodic drumming concept far, and their kits include a whole range of drums and percussion instruments tuned to exact pitches. This allows them to play melodically and rhythmically at the same time.

However, if you have a standard four- or five-piece drum kit you can still practise and play some melodies on your drum kit.

Let's focus on a four-piece kit in order to make it slightly easier. We have the snare, high tom, floor tom and bass drum. Without thinking of any specific pitch just tune your drums so the high tom pitch is higher than the snare, the snare higher than the floor tom and the floor tom higher than the bass drum. This is a fairly widespread tuning method and your kit may already be tuned this way. Ensure that the snare wires are off so you can hear the pitch.

Now start playing around with these four pitches and see if you can play any melody or song that you know on the drums. This is the first step, but most melodies contain more than four notes so we need some creative methods to help us produce more notes without adding additional kit parts.

Manipulating the pitch

As you know, the pressure of the drumhead affects its pitch. Tightening the lugs raises the pitch while loosening them lowers it. To create additional pitches we can manipulate the sound by applying pressure with one hand on the drum head, while playing it with the other hand or stick.

Let's try this on the snare first. Ensure that the snare wires are off, place your left palm and fingers on the left side of the drumhead and apply slight pressure. While holding this pressure play the drum with your right hand and see if you notice any change in the pitch. If this is not significant apply more pressure with the left hand until you hear a difference. Keep playing with your right hand and change the left hand pressure to create various pitches.

If you want to stretch the pitch possibilities of the snare drum even further, place your left hand elbow on the drumhead instead of your palm. Then follow the same process and you will see that using bigger muscles and more weight allows you to push the pitch further. When you feel comfortable with this technique, practise and apply it to the toms.

Playing Triads

This is an advanced concept which is mainly used in jazz drumming. However this can be very effective in many other styles. If you do not have any music theory background you might find this challenging initially, but there are specific products (such as a 'DrumDial') to help with tuning drums to specific pitches.

A triad is a combination of three notes. Let's take the F major triad for example. It consists of these notes: F, A and C. Most jazz drummers will tune the floor tom to a C, the hi tom to F and the snare to A. Check out your favourite jazz drummers and in particular drummers such as Ari Hoenig to continue learn this technique further.

Playing Melodies

Ex. 1 is a four-bar melody using the snare drum, high tom and floor tom. Play it repeatedly on the kit until it flows well. If you managed to tune your kit to an F triad, the melody should be easy to recognise. If not, you may have to make a few tuning adjustments until it sounds clear.

1

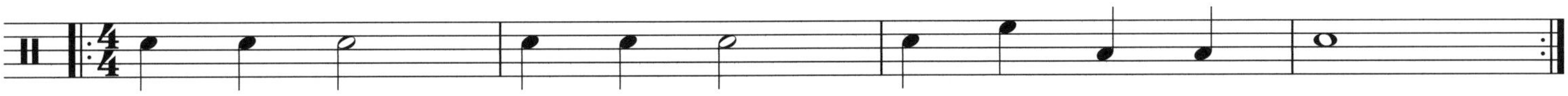

Let's add a few more embellishments to this melody which will make it easier to recognise. Firstly, add a buzz roll on the snare in the fourth bar (remember that the snare wires should be off throughout). Then we will add some pressure with one hand while striking the floor tom in order to raise its pitch slightly. This technique is marked with 'P' for pressure and a curved ascending line next to the note head.

2

Play the melody with these embellishments at the suggested tempo of 110 bpm. By now, I am sure that you recognised it as the beginning of the song 'Jingle Bells'. Once you can play this melody on the kit, use your experience in developing a solo and the steps presented in *Rhythmic Soloing* (p. 24–25) to create your own melodic phrases and solos.

Here are two more examples of well-known melodies that you can play on the drum kit. Develop these into melodic phrases and solos and continue creating your own ideas that will lead to more interesting and individual soloing. (In case you do not recognise them, the answers are printed upside-down at the bottom of this page.)

3

4

3 Old MacDonald **4** Amazing Grace

Ear Training

Play each audio track without looking at the examples below.

After a count-in of four clicks, the two-bar backing is played four times. For the first and third times, listen to the recorded drums. For the second and fourth times, try to play back what you heard.

Finally, refer to the notation below to check whether you recognised the time signature, played back the exercise accurately and understand how it is written.

1

2

3

The following three exercises use the same rhythms as those above, but with the toms as well as the snare drum. The practice concept is the same.

4

5

6

Grooves

You will notice that **Exercises 1–3** are groove based. This means that more parts of the drum kit will be used. This requires secure aural understanding as you will not only have to recognise the rhythms but also the drum voices that are being played.

As explained previously, the backing track will play four times and you should attempt to play back during the second and fourth plays. We will focus on $\frac{4}{4}$, $\frac{7}{4}$ and $\frac{7}{8}$ in these grooves, but feel free to create your own exercises in other time signatures too.

1 ♩= 90 **Funk**

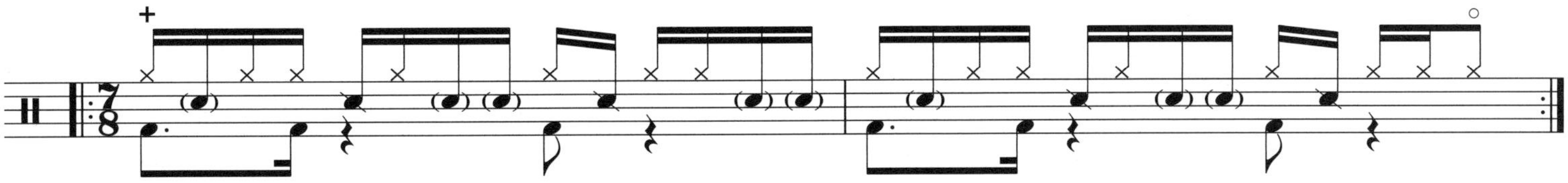

2 ♩= 80 **Metal**

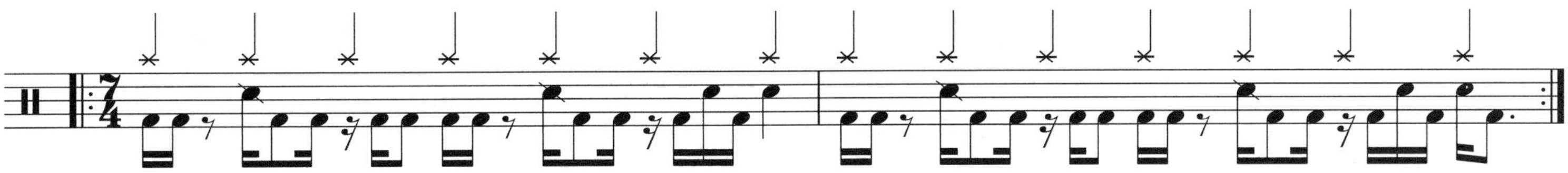

3 ♩= 160 **New Orleans** (slightly swung)

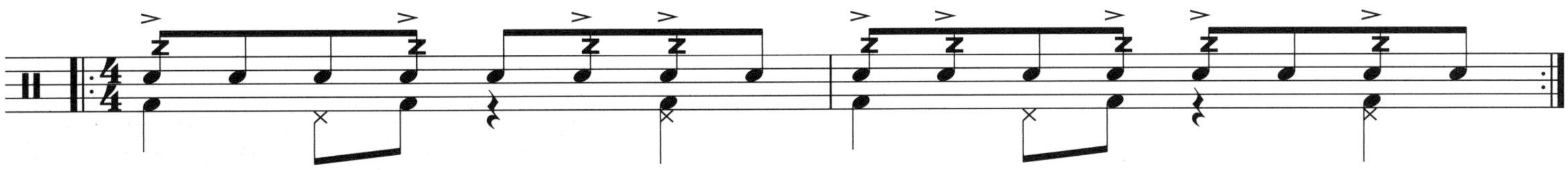

Now, let's take two-bar grooves and place a two-beat fill at the end of the phrase.

See if you can identify all the detail and play them back with conviction.

4 ♩= 90 **Funk**

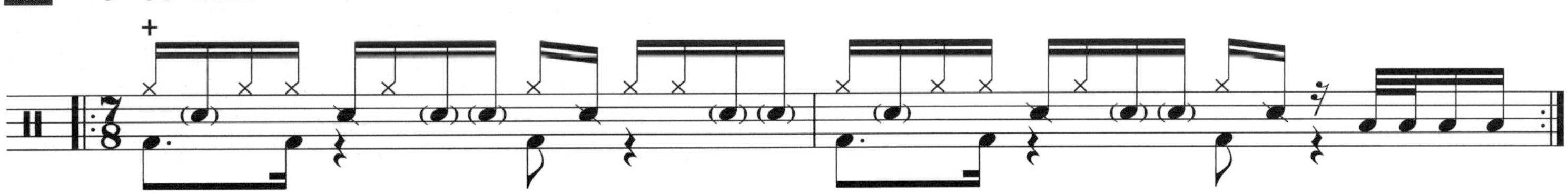

5 ♩= 80 **Metal**

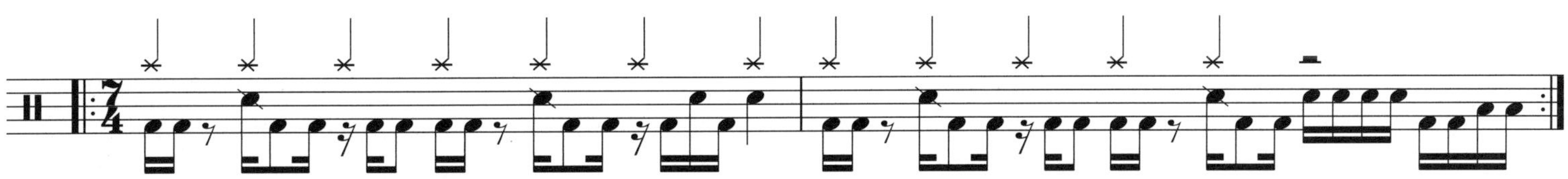

6 ♩= 160 **New Orleans** (slightly swung)

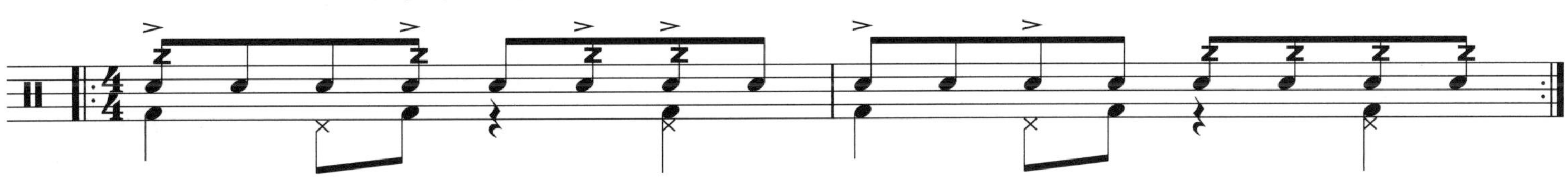

Inspirational Drummers

Buddy Rich

Buddy Rich was an American jazz drummer and bandleader known for his virtuoso technique, power and speed. He inspired generations of drummers and is still regarded by many as the greatest drummer ever.

Buddy Rich was born in Manhattan in 1917 and started playing drums at the age of 18 months. During his early childhood Rich was already a phenomenon and reportedly the second-highest paid child entertainer in the world. At the age of eleven he was amazingly already performing as a bandleader, and working with well known jazz artists by the age of seventeen. Rich was very popular on the jazz scene, both in studio and live situations, working with artists including Artie Shaw, Tommy Dorsey, Benny Carter, Harry James, Frank Sinatra and Oscar Peterson. Rich was also known as a strict but convincing bandleader and performed extensively with his Buddy Rich Big Band worldwide including some classic TV appearances.

Rich generally used the traditional grip with his left hand. He was known for long drum solos while demonstrating stick tricks such as performing a fast roll by slapping two drumsticks together in a circular motion. Rich was known for using Zildjian cymbals (most recently the Avedis series) and Ludwig drums with a five-piece set up including a 24" bass drum, 13" tom, two 16" floor toms and a 14" x 5.5" snare drum.

Before joining Ludwig in the 1970s Rich used drums by Slingerland and Rogers.

Rich died at the age of 69 in 1987 but his legacy lives on. In the mid 1990s there were a number of memorial concerts for Buddy Rich that included performances by Neil Peart, Steve Gadd, Steve Smith, Max Roach and many others. These fantastic performances as well as rare drumming footage of Rich became very popular worldwide and part of today's drumming culture.

Recommended Listening

'Mercy, Mercy, Mercy'
'Love For Sale'
'Groovin' Hard'

Terry Bozzio

Terry Bozzio was born in San Francisco, California in 1950. He is best known for his work with Frank Zappa, Brecker Brothers and Missing Persons.

Bozzio was trained on classical percussion as well as on the drum kit. He regularly played with various bands, orchestras and Baroque chamber ensembles. Bozzio's professional career was launched in 1975 when he joined Frank Zappa's band, The Mothers of Invention. A few years later he joined The Brecker Brothers and as a result became a popular choice for many artists in the 1980s. Bozzio worked with Andy Taylor, Herbie Hancock, Mick Jagger and even made his first ever live appearance on American TV with guitarist Jeff Beck.

After 15 years of professional drumming (1975–1990) Bozzio started to stretch accepted boundaries by developing ostinato-based drum solo compositions. The ostinato is generally played using unorthodox bass drum and hi-hat patterns while soloing against these rhythms using the hands. This has led Bozzio to develop melodic drumming as an integral part of his style, using his background as a pitched percussionist to design a drum kit with two octaves of pitched toms and several tuned cymbals and effects. His most recent setup includes over 25 drums and over 50 cymbals and percussion, allowing him to fuse melodic drumming with conventional rhythmic playing. He has become one of the only drummers in the world to make a career as a solo drummer. This has also resulted in global recognition and placed Bozzio as one of the most innovative educators in the field.
One of Bozzio's most recent projects is an improvisational instrumental supergroup called HoBoLeMa. Apart from Bozzio the group consists of guitarist Allan Holdsworth, bassist Tony Levin and percussionist Pat Mastelotto. They are still developing their improvisational concepts and performing live around the world.

Recommended Listening

'The Black Page'
***Solos & Duets* (with Chad Wackerman)**
***Terry Bozzio live with the Tosca Strings* (DVD)**

Joey Jordison

Joey Jordison is known as one of the most unique and inspiring metal drummers in the world. In 2010 Jordison was voted the best drummer of the past 25 years by readers of Rhythm magazine, ahead of legends such as Mike Portnoy, Dave Grohl and Neil Peart. Jordison started drumming at the age of eight, having played the guitar and gained an appreciation for music from a very early age. He has always had a passion for speed drumming and has continued to set up various bands in order to develop this skill in a musical context. After playing with many local bands Jordison joined the heavy metal band Slipknot in 1995. With Slipknot he recorded, toured and produced for

18 successful years, during which the band pioneered the new wave of American heavy metal. Jordison became a global drumming icon. Slipknot released many big-selling and award-winning albums during their career as well as four platinum-selling live DVDs. Jordison was replaced in 2013, but the new drummer's identity has never been confirmed as all members of Slipknot wear masks throughout all gigs and public appearances. According to rumour the new drummer is Jay Weinberg.

Jordison has also worked with Korn, Rob Zombie, Otep, Satyricon as well as producing, playing guitar and remixing various musical projects. His most recent band Scar the Martyr released their first album in 2013. Jordison has worked with cymbal manufacturer Paiste since 2001 to develop the Black Alpha Hyper series. The cymbals in this line contain nine tribal-S logos and have a black coating. On the drum kit front, Jordison has had a successful and long relationship with Pearl, most noticeably developing a unique all-steel snare drum, most notably the JJ-1355.

Recommended Listening

'Duality'
'Psychosocial'
'Snuff'

Style Focus: Metal

Stylistic Fills

Fast metal fills played between grooves are an important aspect of metal drumming and especially Jordison's style. On this page we will explore a few ideas that can help you develop fills of this type and incorporate them into your playing.

Most metal drummers use a double bass drum pedal or two bass drums. If you already have this in your setup you should find this lesson very interesting. If you do not have a double bass drum pedal at this stage consider getting one as it will immensely strengthen your left foot. You can try to adapt the grooves and fills in this lesson to be played with one bass drum but you may lose some stylistic flavour as well as struggle to get these to very high speeds.

Ex. 1 addresses changing rhythms with the double bass drum while playing repetitive phrases with the hands. The key is ensuring that when playing 32nd notes with the hands and feet there are no unintended flams and everything synchronises well.

1 ♩ = 90

The next exercise combines rhythmic displacement with rim shot accents and six 32nd-note bass drums to finish.

2 ♩ = 90

Metal fills often combine phrases of two and four strokes with double bass drum strokes in order to move swiftly around the kit. The balance between the feet and hands is crucial here.

3 ♩ = 90

Blast Beats

The stylistic metal grooves called blast beats are another integral part of the metal style. These beats originated in performances by jazz drummers such as Tony Williams and Sunny Murray from the fifties to the seventies but in the eighties developed with more of a modern approach in the UK punk and hardcore music scene. Blast beats include constant strokes on the hi-hat, snare and bass drum. The hi-hat pattern can also be played on the crash cymbal, ride cymbal or even a china cymbal.

Blast beats are generally played with the double bass drum (as notated) but can also be played with one bass drum.

Ex. 1 is the *hammer blast*. Try this slowly and work on accuracy before speeding up. Notice that the hammer blast is based on unison between the hands and feet. When you feel comfortable with this blast try it in triplet eighth notes too.

1 ♩=80

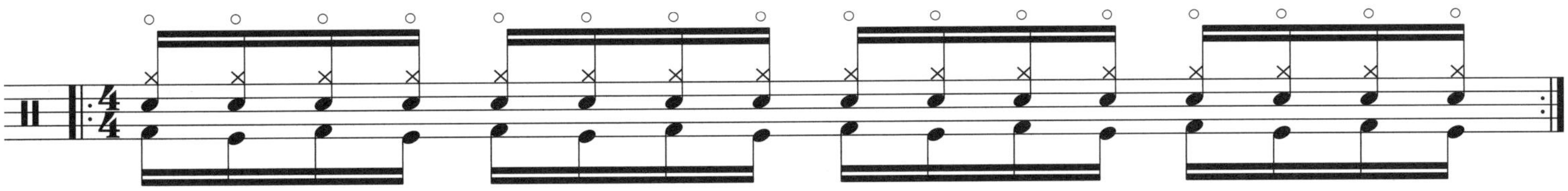

The traditional blast is notated in Ex 2. Here we alternate between the bass drum and snare. This can also be played with the snare first.

When you feel comfortable with this groove try to gradually raise the speed. This blast will also be effective in sextuplets.

2 ♩= 80

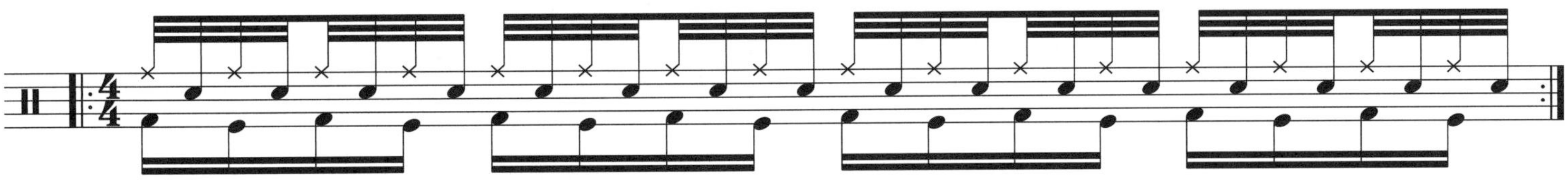

Ex. 3 is a good way of developing the technique and balance required for a solid traditional blast. Focus on controlled movement and keep breathing. The best blast beats drummers in the world all say that developing the ability to remain calm while playing a super fast blast beat is the key to this style. As always, try this with various sticking options (singles starting with each hand, doubles, paradiddles).

3 ♩= 80

Ex. 4 shows another important blast: the skank blast, which is actually the predecessor of the two blasts presented above. When you feel comfortable with the three blasts try to put them together with the fills on p. 60. Aim to move between the blast beats smoothly and use the fills in between. Keep the pulse consistent and practise with a time limit to develop your stamina and endurance.

4

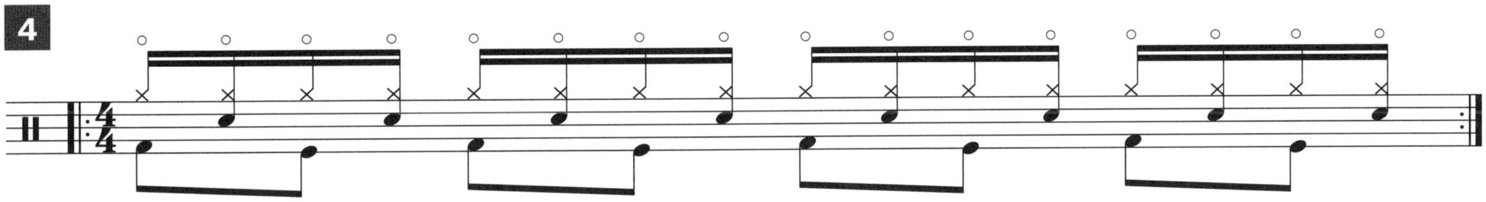

Piece Preparation: 'Blast Monster'

This is a metal piece in the style of Joey Jordison, Derek Roddy and Dave Lombardo. The backing track of 'Blast Monster' can be downloaded for free from **www.vvinner.com/downloads**.

Double Bass Drum

Some of the grooves and fills in this piece include double bass drum parts. If you like playing metal and followed this series from earlier levels you will probably have a double bass drum pedal in your setup by now, and you should find the patterns in this piece authentically stylistic. If you do not have a double bass drum pedal yet and still want to perform this piece you will need to make some changes to the part, either playing the double bass drum pattern with one bass drum, omitting a few bass drums as necessary or even attempting creative variations as shown in **Ex. 1**.

A Intro

The intro is divided into four-bar sections. In these four bars you have a two-bar metal fill and two bars of blast beat. Fills of this type and the basic blasts are explained in detail on p. 61. The most important element is accuracy and balance between hands and feet.

B Verse

The verse has a four-bar groove that repeats four times with some variations. This is a half time groove where we only have one backbeat snare in each bar. This is usually played on the third beat, however in each third bar in the sequence the back beat snare is played one eighth note later. Focus on using the open hi-hat as your anchor so the bass drum and snare variations do not effect your sense of time. Another stylistic variation to explore with this type of groove is changing from quarter notes on the hi-hat to playing only beats 1 and 3 on the crash (**Ex. 2**). This will also be very effective if played on the china cymbal.

C Chorus

In the chorus groove you will need to utilise the double bass drum skills you have developed throughout this series. We suggest you break this section down and practise individual patterns first. You will notice that most bars won't have a bass drum on the first beat but on the offbeat instead. In order to play this type of groove with conviction your technique, coordination and sense of pulse must be very strong. If the feet pattern sounds uneven, break it down to individual bars and practise at slower tempos. Use a metronome with sixteenth note subdivision to help you play accurately.

The chorus section is in $\frac{4}{4}$, however there is one bar with a drum fill in the time signature of $\frac{3}{4}$. This means that there are only three quarter notes in this bar but from the next bar the time signature returns to $\frac{4}{4}$. This can be challenging and feel like the groove has 'turned'. We suggest counting the beats (1 2 3) when you get to this bar until this feels natural.

The final fill in this section includes consistent sixteenth notes with both hands and both feet. When performing a fill like this we suggest using alternate sticking and starting with the leading hand and foot. If you want to stretch your technique and coordination, try the following ideas which are also detailed in **Ex. 3**:

Vary the sticking

a) Doubles
b) Single paradiddle
c) RRRR LLLL
d) Your own sticking patterns

Cross Coordination

Start with your leading hand and following foot and vice versa. This is known as cross coordination.

D Guitar Solo

The first guitar solo includes a stylistic type of groove that shows advanced control of time. The crash cymbal plays consistent eighth notes with accented quarter notes while the bass and snare play what feels like a $\frac{5}{4}$ pattern over the $\frac{4}{4}$ crash pattern. With grooves like this it is crucial that you know exactly where each beat lands in order to perform with conviction whether playing with a backing track or a live band. Do not forget to adapt your counting whenever the time signature changes in the notation.

In the second groove of this section we have another stylistic way of creating a different rhythmic feel over the $\frac{4}{4}$ time signature. The implied feel is of a $\frac{3}{4}$ time signature. Have a look at **Ex. 4** and see how three bars of $\frac{4}{4}$ fits 4 cycles of the implied $\frac{3}{4}$ groove. This concept will be explained further on p. 88–89.

E Drum Solo

The drum solo in this piece connects the guitar solo and the D.C. which sends you back to the beginning of the piece. The solo is 16 bars long so you have time to develop your ideas to the intensity needed when returning to the hectic opening section. Listen to the backing track without playing first and understand the rhythmic riff played by the guitar and bass. Then, try to play phrases that go with and against the riff. Finally, construct your own improvisation ideas and use the riff as your support.

If you find that the speed of the piece makes this solo very challenging, try to use different types of rhythm and allow more space between your phrases. Another useful tool is setting the metronome (or programmed loop) to a slightly higher tempo (up to 5 bpm faster than the original) and practising your improvisation ideas. When you feel comfortable at the faster tempo, gradually drop it down to the original tempo and mentally this should now feel easier to perform.

1

2

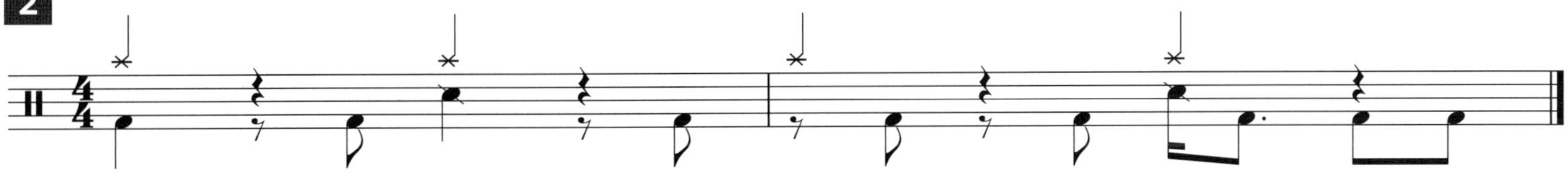

3

4

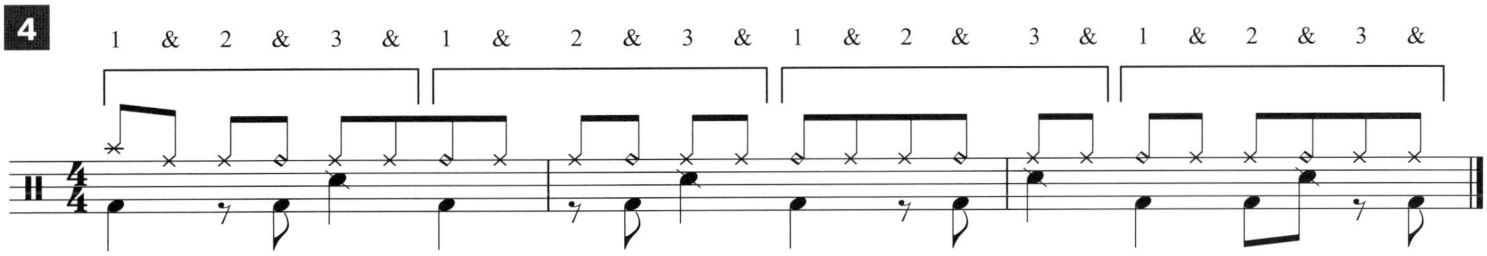

'Blast Monster'

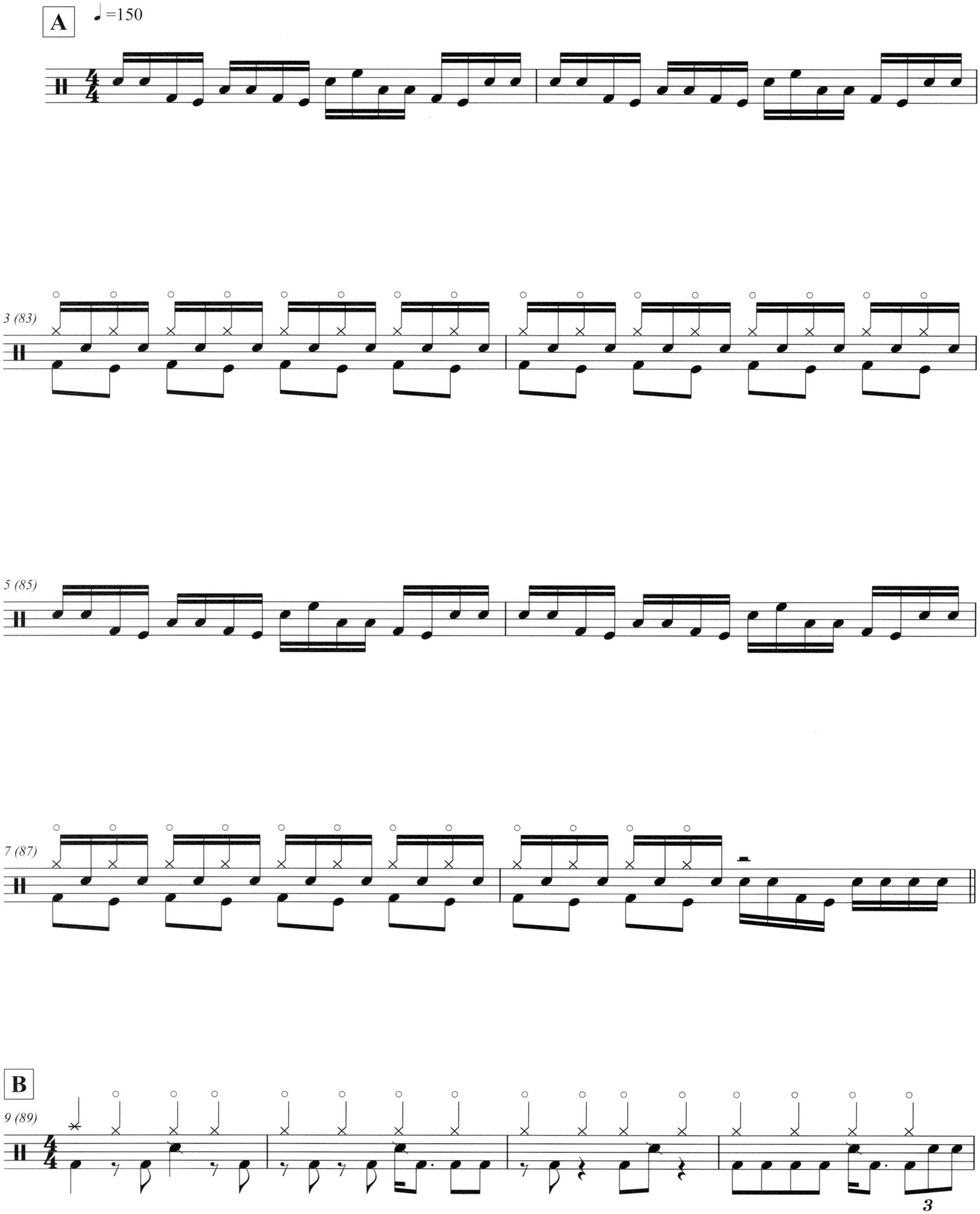

13 (93)
3
3
17 (97)
3
21 (101)
To Coda
C
25
29

33
2
37
2
3
4
41
4
4
45
47

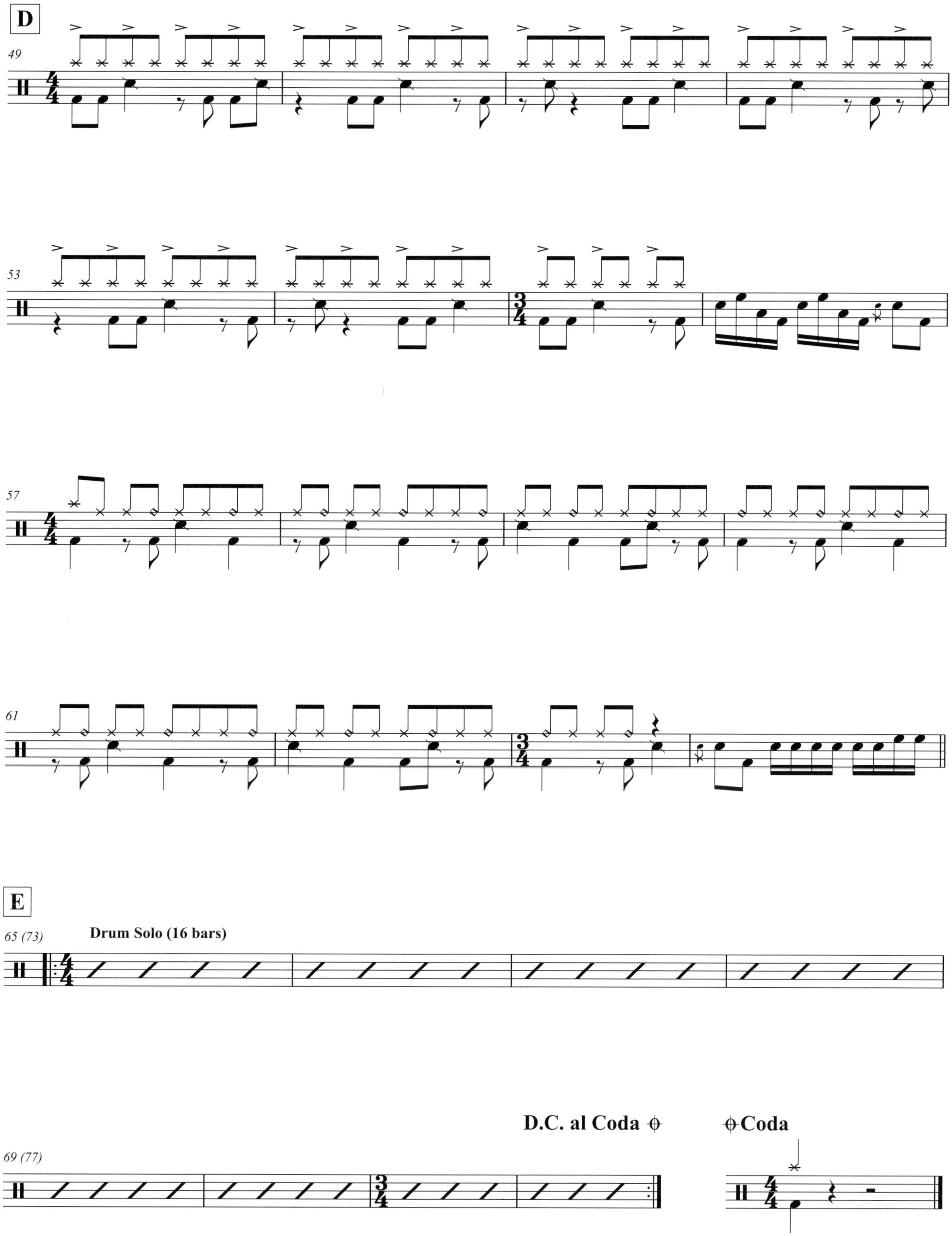
D
49
53
57
61
E
65 (73)
Drum Solo (16 bars)
69 (77)
D.C. al Coda
Coda

Fingers Technique and Rudiments

Fingers Technique

The basic fingers technique was explained in Level 2. To recap: the concept involves utilising your finger muscles to bounce the stick. As with all advanced techniques, we aim to achieve the movement naturally and with minimum effort. Ensure that your fulcrum is secure and the fingers are moving together as a unit. Fingers technique is also a vital part of advanced techniques such as the Moeller Technique (see p .38).

In **Ex. 1** below we will aim to strengthen each one of the four fingers: index, middle, ring finger and pinky individually. This technique has been very effectively demonstrated by Jojo Mayer. Start with your right hand, focus on securing your fulcrum and ensuring that your hand is not tense so the stick can move freely.

Use the index finger in order to help the stick bounce on the pad or drum. Practise this for a few minutes until it feels more comfortable. Next, use the middle finger as the 'engine' of the movement, then the ring finger and finally the pinky. Notice that certain fingers are naturally stronger while others might be more flexible. The main aim is to maintain good posture, relax and allow the stick to do the work for you.

Now, try playing consistent strokes using your fingers but changing the finger creating the movement every eight strokes. This exercise can be developed endlessly with different finger combinations. If you use this concept and practise **Ex. 1** and similar exercises daily, your finger control and overall technique will improve beyond anything you thought yourself capable of.

1

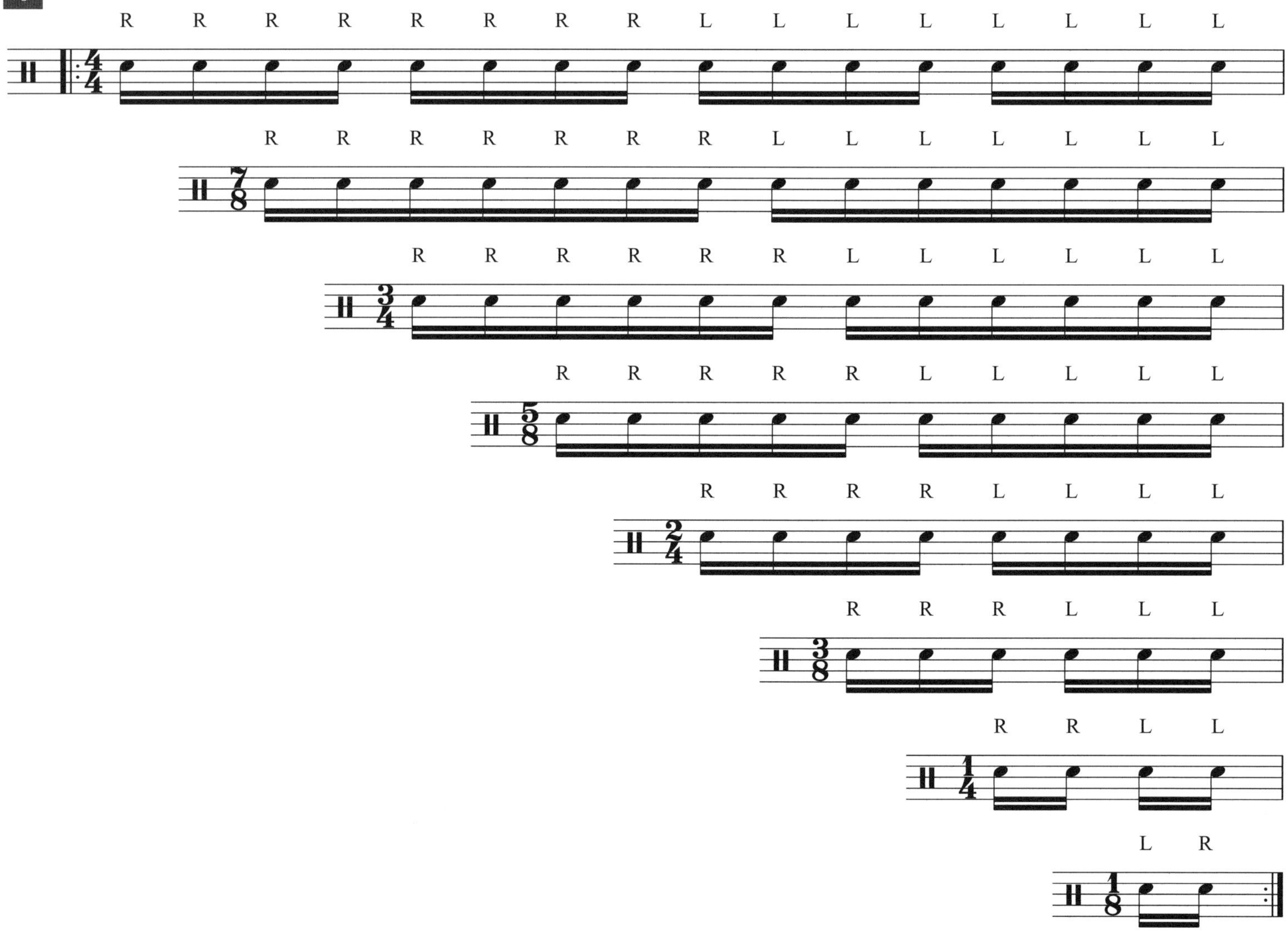

Rudiments

Hybrid Ratamacue

This is a challenging fusion of the single, double and triple ratamacue.
Be sure to try some musical applications of this rudiment around the kit.

1

Swiss Army Triplet

This rudiment is very effective when used on the drum kit as it helps you move more freely around the kit and play more interesting voicing because of the flams. The specified sticking will assist you in playing these very fast as long as you understand the timing and pattern of each hand. Ensure that all grace notes are soft.

2

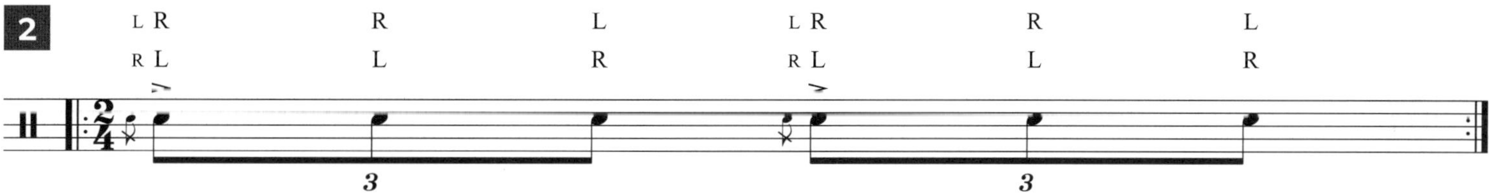

Hybrid Rolls

Now that you know how to play various roll rudiments, you should try putting them together in various ways. Here is one example for a hybrid roll phrase in $\frac{5}{4}$ that includes ten, eleven and thirteen stroke rolls with suggested sticking.

3

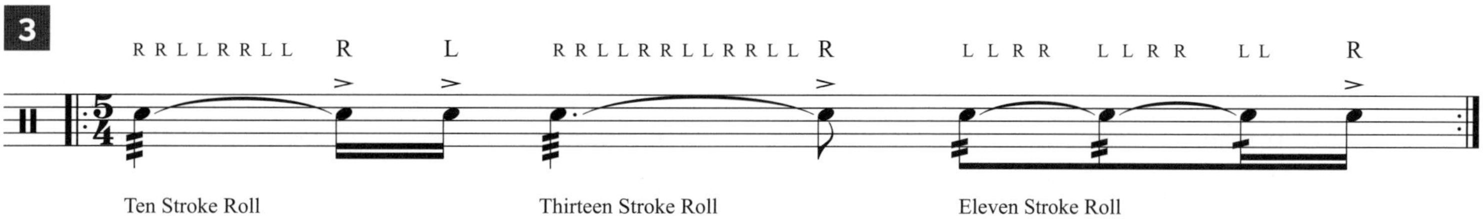

Advanced Hi-Hat Techniques

Splashed Hi-Hat

The basics of this technique were introduced earlier in this book (Samba Grooves, p. 21). If necessary refer back to remind yourself how to perform this technique correctly.

In this lesson we will take this further and try to reach maximum control with this interesting sound. Practise **Ex. 1A** and **1B** and focus on the accuracy and correct length of the open hi-hat.

1A ♩ = 80

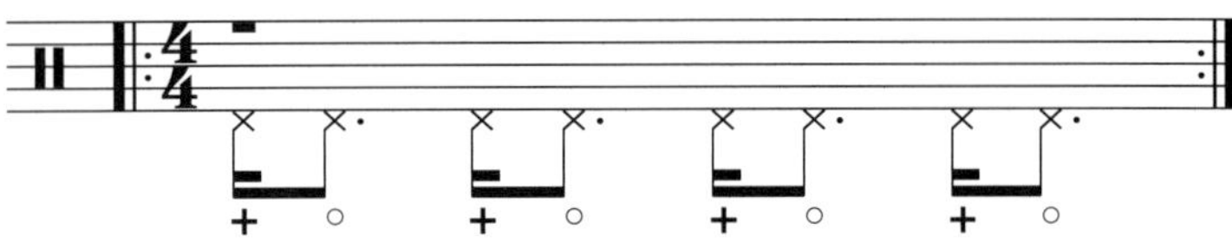

1B

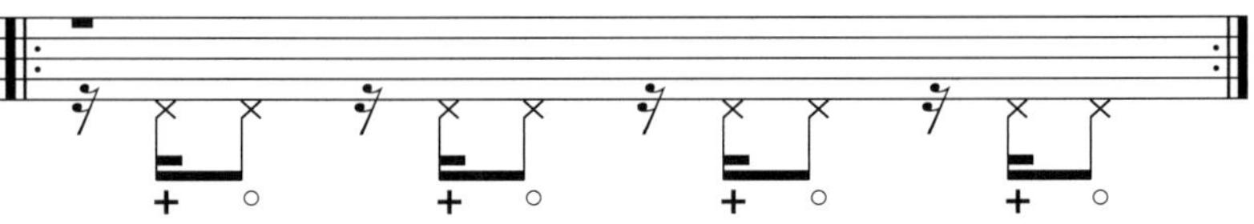

Now let's look at a funky groove with splashed off beat hi-hats. Remember that all sixteenth notes should be swung in this type of groove.

2 ♩ = 80 Swung 16s

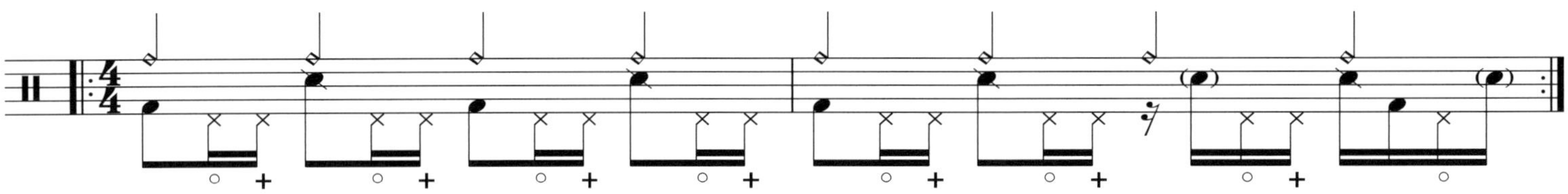

In **Ex. 3A** and **3B** we have musical phrases with the splashed and closed hi-hat sound. Practise these until you feel comfortable before incorporating a splashed hi-hat pattern like this into a groove such as **Ex. 4**.

Develop this and test your coordination by creating busier bass drum and snare patterns, then experiment with adding this sound to your favourite grooves as well as soloing over an ostinato with splashed hi-hat.

3A ♩ = 80

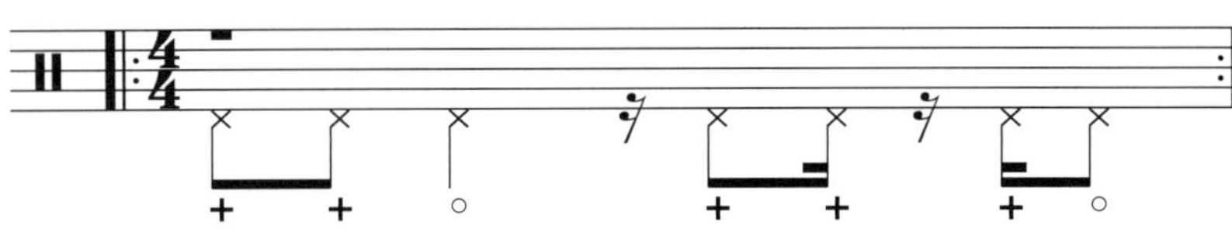

3B

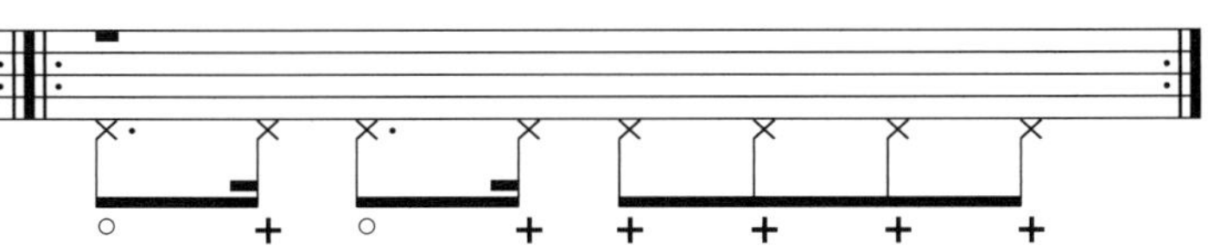

4 ♩ = 80

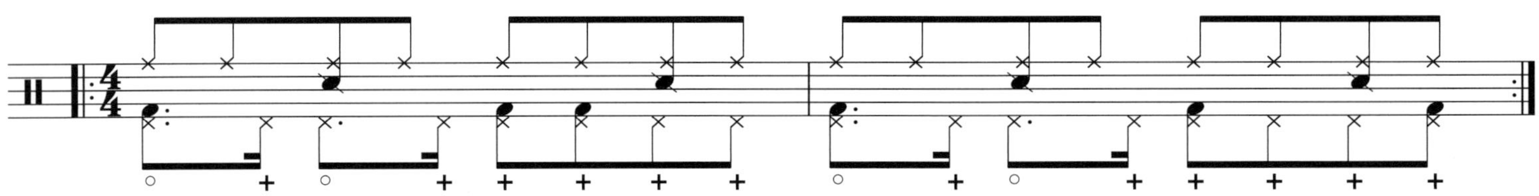

Stepped Hi-Hat

This term refers to playing the hi-hat with the foot. The stepped hi-hat sound is snappier than the sound produced when hitting the hi-hat with the stick. This is important, as producing different sounds from the kit will make you a versatile drummer. Try to open the hi-hat cymbals slightly more than usual to produce a convincing stepped hi-hat sound. This is not a completely new technique but using it within grooves can be challenging at first, mainly because it requires left foot control. When you understand the concept try incorporating this new technique into your playing.

1

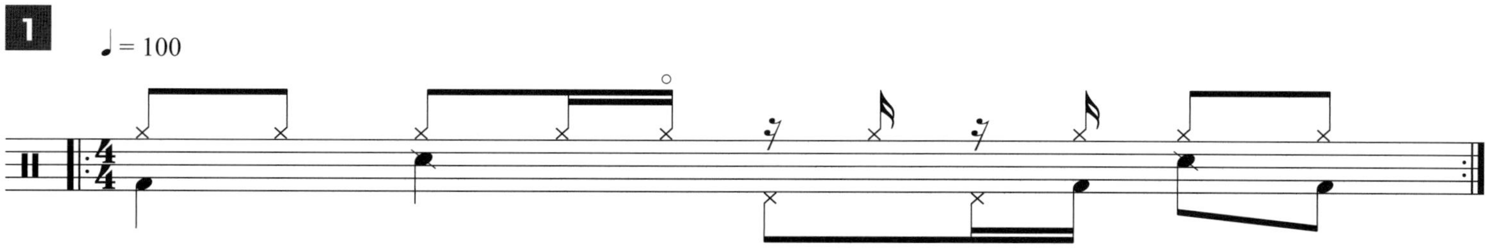

2

Left Hand Hi-Hat Flick

The idea of this technique is to embellish the hi-hat pattern in grooves with a quick left hand stroke. The left hand that plays the snare backbeat will have to move between the snare and hi-hat in the most efficient way. This means travelling underneath the right hand. Initially, this can feel awkward and there is a good chance that you will hit the sticks together while getting used to it but with time this can become very useful and add spice to many of the grooves you already know. Here are a few funk and gospel grooves using this technique.

3

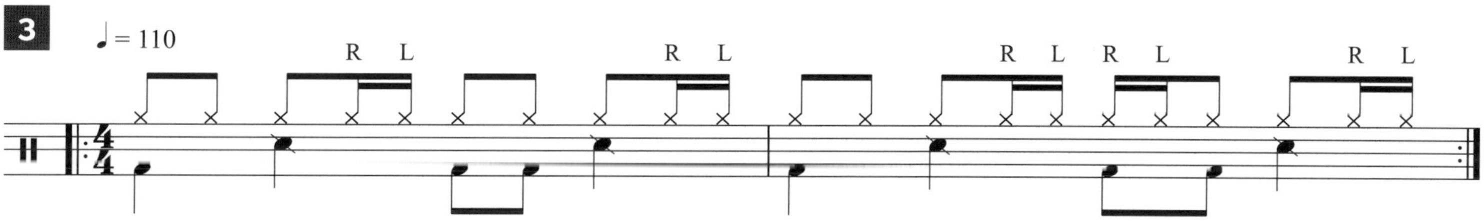

4

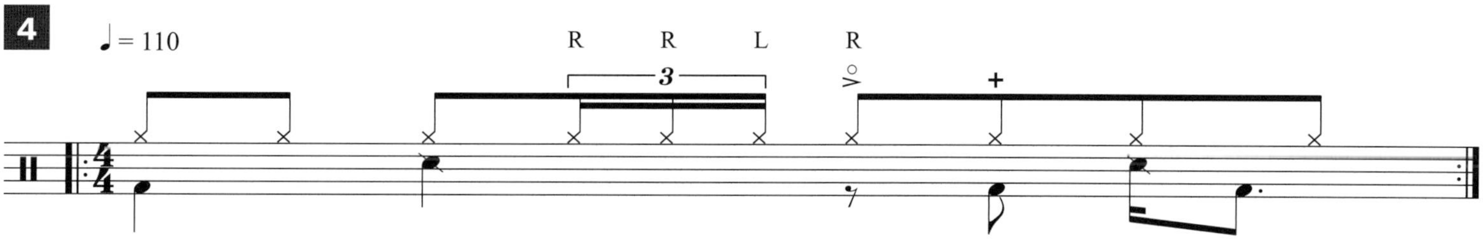

5

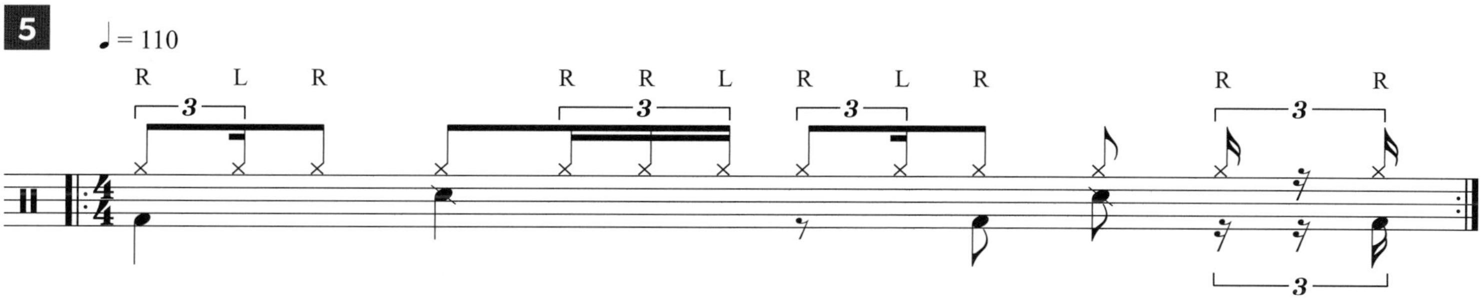

Brushes

Constant Swoosh

Hopefully by this stage you have experimented with the variety of sticks, beaters and brushes that are available. Each type of beater offers a certain sound, colour and dynamic level. Many of them can be used with similar grip to the normal sticks with minor adjustments, mainly because the weight of the beater will vary. Brushes are technically more complex but offer many possible musical directions. We will explore the basic brushes techniques in this lesson while focusing on jazz grooves. There are many types of brushes nowadays and it is simply a case of experimenting to find which works best for you and your music. The grooves shown here will be most effective with traditional wire brushes.

The first and most important concept for playing brushes is the constant swoosh as it allows you to create various note lengths. The swoosh is created by playing the brushes on the snare drum while maintaining constant contact with the drumhead. Practice circular motions with the brushes at a comfortable tempo such as 70 bpm. Most drummers combine a clockwise left hand motion with an anticlockwise right hand motion. You can of course choose to reverse this if you think it will work better with your technique. Ensure that the brushes do not clash and each motion lasts exactly one beat. Aim for a relaxed and smooth motion with both hands following a consistent pulse. Practise this for at least ten minutes a day until it feels solid. In **Ex. 2** below we add the hi-hat foot backbeat as well as a light backbeat accent with both hands.

1

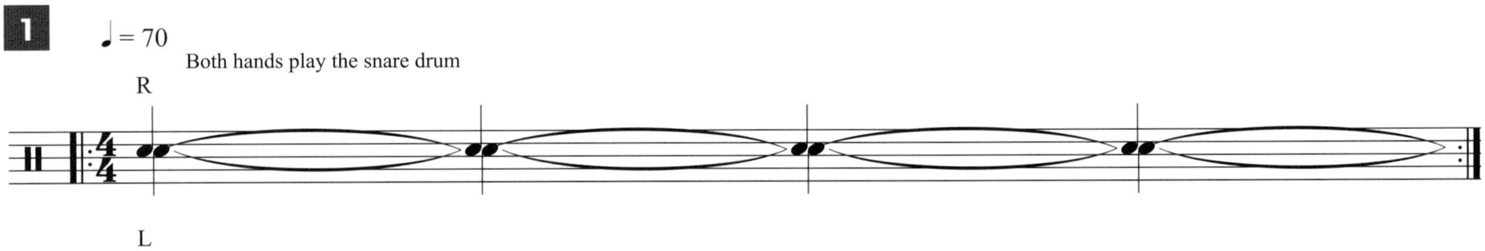

2

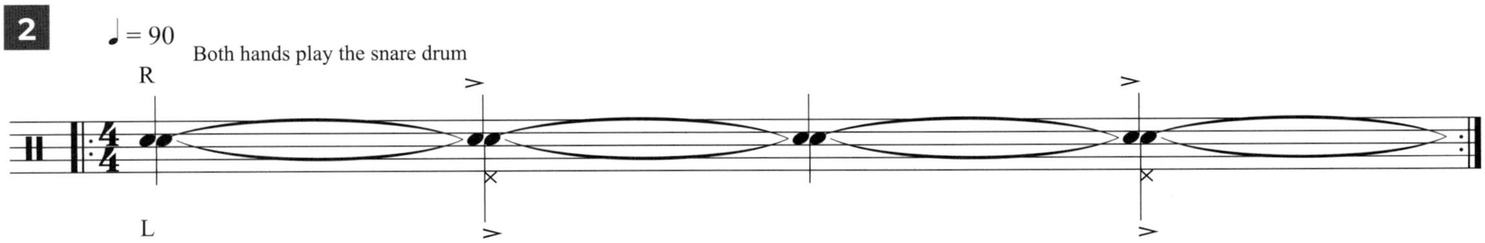

Jazz Groove

Here is an example of a basic jazz groove using brushes. The left hand does the swoosh motion and the right hand plays the jazz ride cymbal pattern on the snare. You will need to adjust the movement so that the hands do not clash. This can be effective at many tempos, but be aware that the faster you go the smaller the circular swoosh motion gets.

Alternatively, the swoosh motion can cover two beats rather than one as shown below. In **Ex. 4** there is a similar groove that explores using the swoosh sound with your right hand as part of the swing pattern. You can also play with the right hand on the ride cymbal as an alternative. Try adding the hi-hat foot on beats 2 and 4 when you feel ready.

3

4

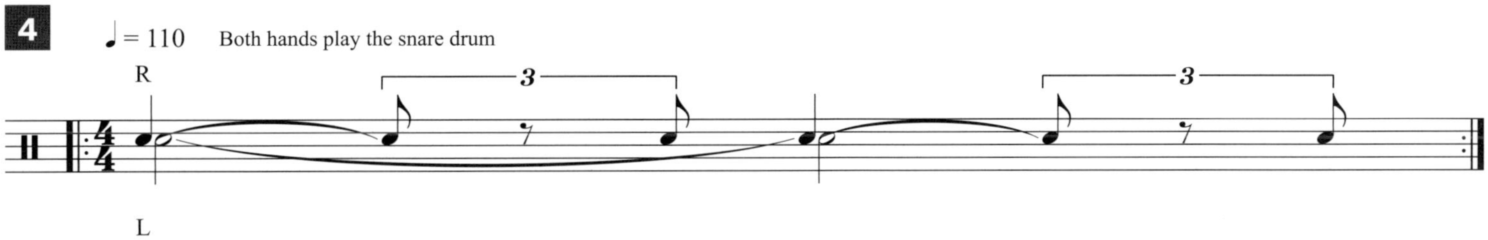

Latin Groove

Brushes can be used for effective and impressive Latin grooves. This technique is suitable for slow or mid-tempo bossa nova grooves but can also be used for samba with some adjustments.

The right hand plays a combination of one beat swoosh and two taps. The direction of the movement of the brush can be adjusted – experiment and see what works and sounds best according to your technique.

Practise this separately until it feels comfortable, then add the bossa nova clave with the left hand and the standard bossa feet pattern (**Ex. 6**). The left hand can use a brush or a stick with the cross stick sound. Try different tempos and vary the pressure of the brush until you decide how you want to articulate the pattern.

5

6

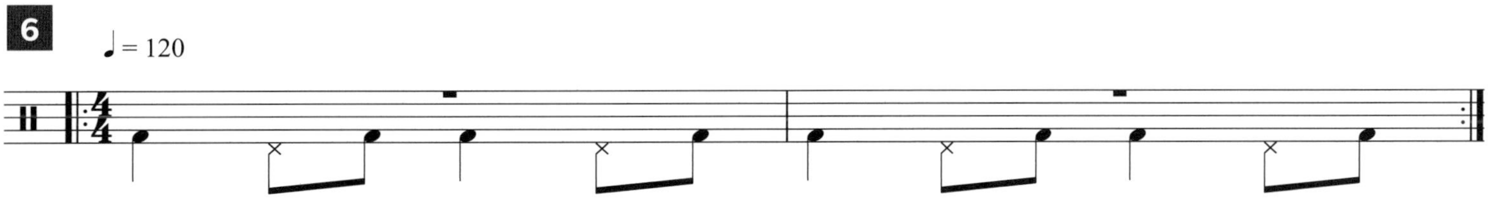

Odd Time Signatures

We have already encountered grooves in five and seven. In this lesson we will explore more advanced odd time signatures. The best way to get comfortable with grooves like this is to play them consistently over a period of time. You can use the metronome initially but this can become boring. A better alternative would be to program a simple loop that is both rhythmically supportive and musical. If you already play in a band and it is musically appropriate, try composing a new song based on an odd time signature groove together with your band members.

> **Tip!**
>
> *Check out these tracks in odd time signatures:*
>
> *Genesis: 'Turn It On Again'* ($\frac{13}{4}$)
> *The Allman Brothers Band: 'Whipping Post'* ($\frac{11}{4}$)
> *Led Zeppelin: 'The Crunge'* ($\frac{9}{8}$)

1

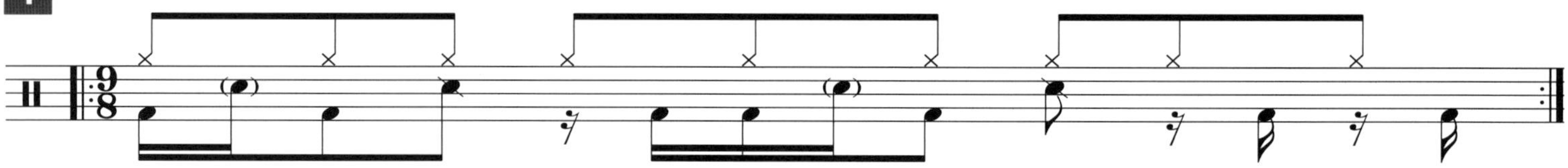

2

3

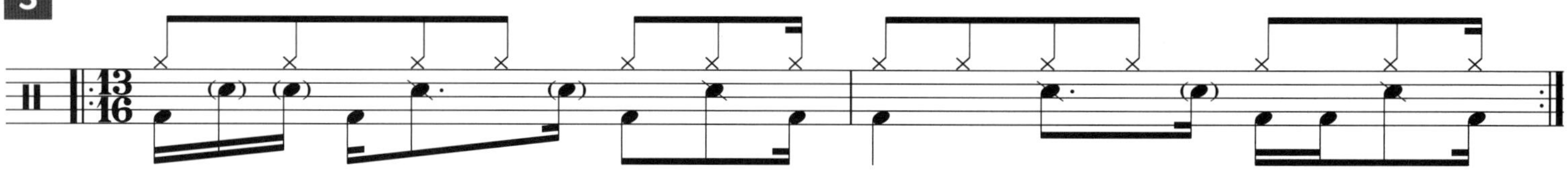

4

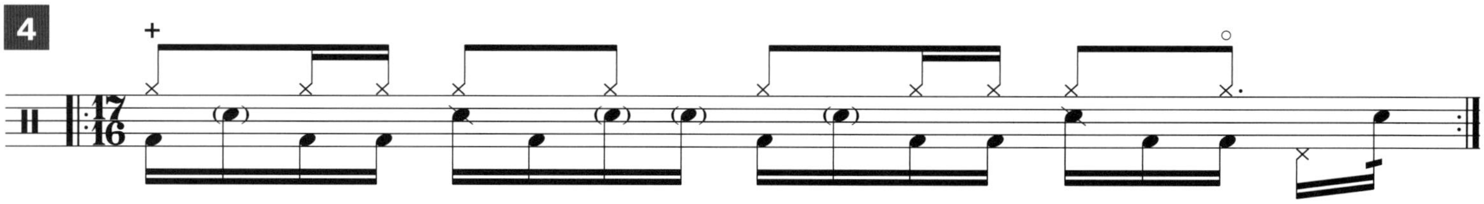

Polymeter

The polyrhythm concept (p. 44–45) is often used with odd time signatures. The polymeter concept is slightly different as it uses different groupings (rather than different rhythms) to enhance the phrase.

The groupings will be implied by using accents or different voicings. In **Ex. 1** the bass drum and snare play in $\frac{4}{4}$ while the ride cymbal implies groupings of three. Both rhythms repeat on the '1' every three bars.

1

In **Ex. 2** the ride cymbal pattern implies five while the bass drum and snare hold the $\frac{4}{4}$. The rhythms sync on the first beat of every fifth bar, or ten quarter note beats as in **Ex. 2**.

2

Ex. 3 applies the polymeter concept to an odd time signature groove. In this groove the hi-hat and snare hold a solid $\frac{5}{4}$ rock pattern while the bass drum implies groupings of three.

3

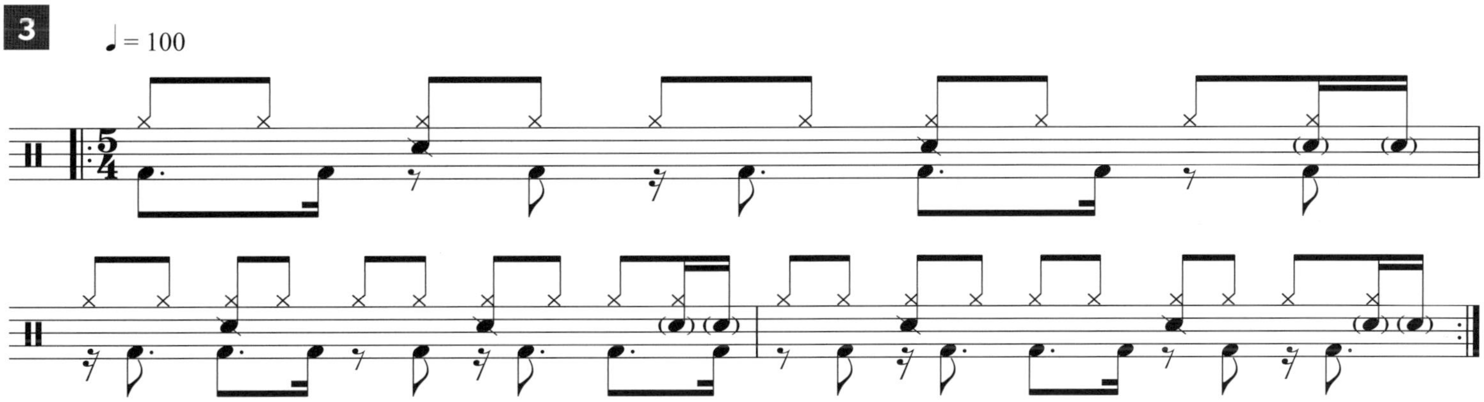

Salsa

The Clave

Salsa, like almost all Afro-Cuban music, is based on repetitive rhythmic patterns known as *clave*. The two main claves that you will need to know are the Son Clave and Rumba Clave. Each of these can be played as 2:3 or as 3:2. These numbers refer to the number of hits per bar.

Practise **Ex. 1–4** by playing on any chosen drum, cymbal or even tapping your hand or your foot with a metronome. Salsa music is usually written in *cut time* (¢). This can also be written as $\frac{2}{2}$ and is like $\frac{4}{4}$, but the feel and counting of the groove are in half time. Put on some quality Salsa music and tap along to it until you feel familiar with these four claves.

1 Son Clave 2:3

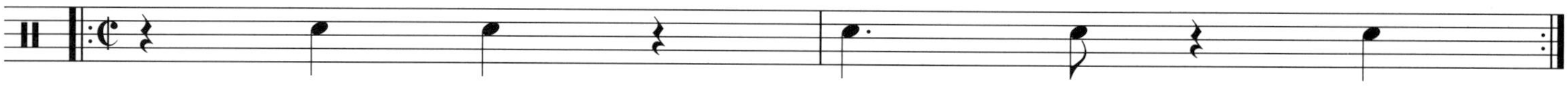

2 Son Clave 3:2

3 Rumba Clave 2:3

4 Rumba Clave 3:2

Here is an example of the Son Clave 2:3 in a Salsa groove. The clave is played with the cross stick snare and the ride cymbal will play the leading pattern also known as *cascara*.

We will use one of the common feet patterns of this style of drumming. Once you feel confident with this groove make adjustments so you can play all four claves above within a groove.

5 Son Clave 2:3 Groove

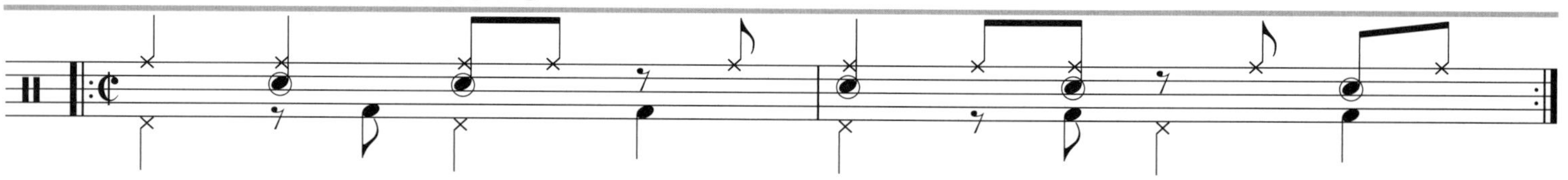

Tip!

Check out these Afro-Cuban drummers:

Horacio Hernandez
Robby Ameen
Alex Acuña

Songo

Modern Salsa drum grooves try to combine many patterns of traditional Cuban percussion instruments. These include congas, timbales, bongos, guiro and claves. The Songo groove is one of the best known modern adaptation of salsa for the drum kit.

1

The hi-hat foot is another musical addition you might wish to consider. In **Ex. 2**, notice that the splashed hi-hat is also used.

Now try the replacing the hi-hat sound with the bell of the ride cymbal or cowbell.

2

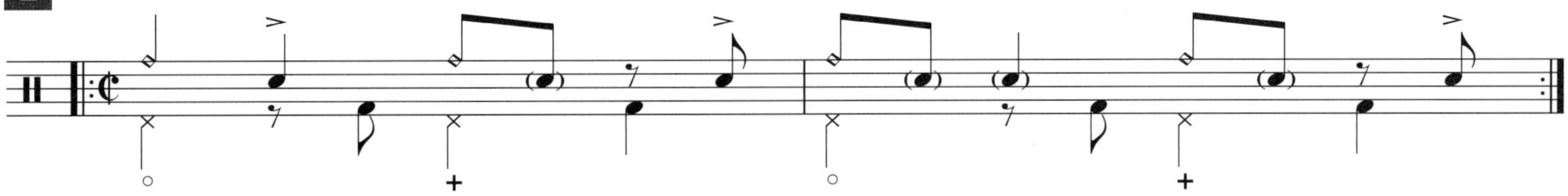

Stylistic Sound

Once you feel comfortable with salsa grooves and advanced four-way coordination, it is time to consider adding stylistic sounds to your kit. Firstly, cascara patterns can be played on the ride bell, cowbell, woodblock and even the rim of any of the drums. Splashed hi-hat can be used as part of the hi-hat pattern. A more advanced concept: change the pattern and play the clave with your left foot.

Having mastered this with all four claves, you will have one hand free to add more texture. The foot clave can be played with the hi-hat but a foot cowbell or foot woodblock would be more efficient. **Ex. 3** shows a songo groove with the hi-hat foot emphasising the 3:2 rumba clave. Try creating your own variations and play along to your favourite salsa music in order to get the feel right.

3

Electronica

Electronica drum grooves have been developed on the acoustic kit over the past decade. The process of imitating a drum machine or drum loop is known by many drummers as *reverse engineering*.

We will look into adding electronic elements and sounds into the kit on p. 79. The exercises below demonstrate how electronica grooves can be adapted for the acoustic kit. This should be both interesting and challenging.

1 Trip Hop

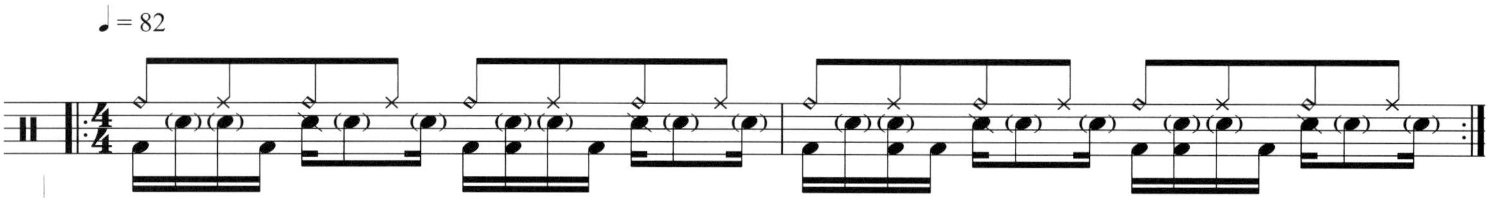

2 Big Beat

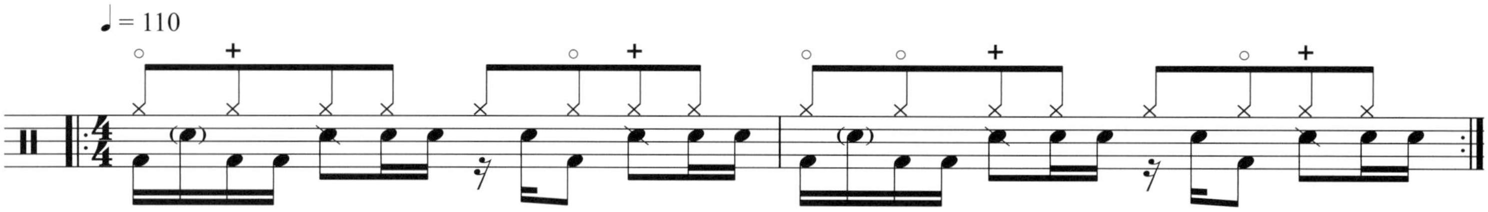

3 Downtempo

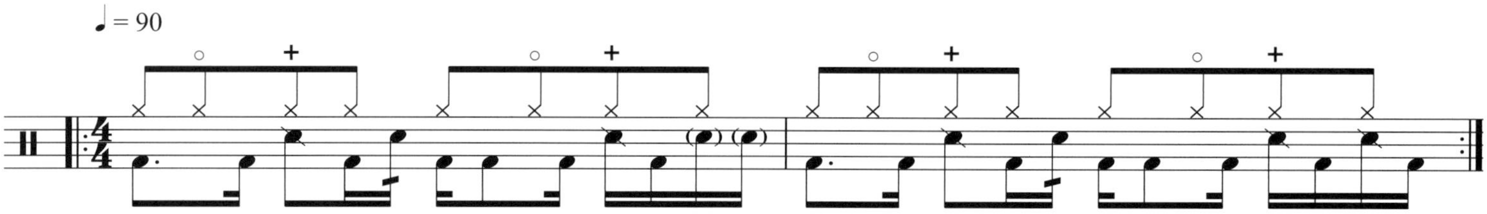

4 House

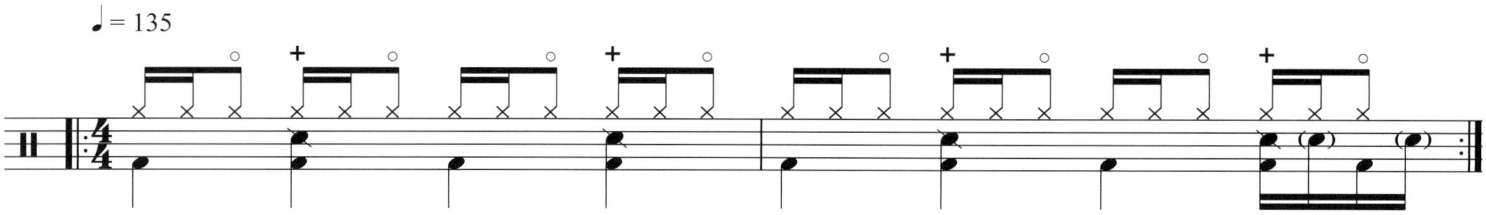

5 Drum and Bass

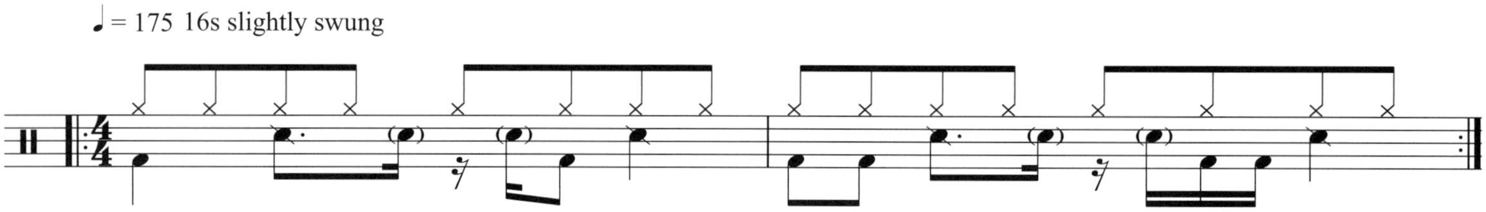

Hybrid Drumming

The term hybrid drumming is a relatively new term in the drumming world.

It refers to using a combination of acoustic drums and cymbals as well as electronic sounds. There are a few ways of incorporating electronic sounds into your setup. Firstly, you will need to understand what each option can achieve, then review and decide what will work best for you in each musical context you are working in.

Drum Pads vs. Triggers

Triggers

These little electronic devices can be clamped to any acoustic drum in your set. Every time you hit the drum, the trigger senses it and plays the electronic sound that you have assigned to it. Triggers are generally used to enhance stylistic bass drum and snare sounds but can also be used to produce any additional colour or sound required. Remember that you will only be able to hear the trigger sounds once connected to an amplifier or PA system.

Drum Pads

Electronic drum pads offer the same possibilities as triggers, but can be played directly. The sensitivity of these pads has been an issue for drummers for years, however the development of technology in this field has resulted in very precise and easy to use drum and cymbal pads. Multi-pad units are another popular option that offers a combination of pads that can be played on, the ability to add external pads or triggers and the ability to store sounds.

Assigning Sounds

Triggers and drum pads are individual devices and on their own do not allow you to save sounds or sets of sounds, so you will either need a computer in your setup or a drum module to control these devices. Most modules come with a basic database of sounds and the ability to save and add many more to make your setup sound individual.

Research what is available on the market and decide what will work best for you. Whatever you choose should be practical and easy to transport to gigs.

Going Hybrid

Going hybrid is something that every drummer should at least consider. It might not be the right thing for the style of music that you are currently playing, however it is a skill that can be utilised in many styles. Moreover, when working with professional productions, the artist or musical director might request that you blend some of the original drum sounds from the album onto your kit, so it is good to be prepared.

The best hybrid setup is one that will suit your style and provide you with everything you need for the future. If you learn how to use it and how to adapt it, changing the sounds for each new musical project should not be difficult.

Musical Direction

Depending on your musical taste and where you want to go with your drumming, going hybrid can actually offer many more possibilities as the triggered sounds do not have to be drums or percussion related. You can decide to trigger any bass guitar sound, keyboard sound, vocal phrase or even a loop (repeated phrase). This opens a whole range of musical possibilities.

Although drummers such as Neil Peart and Danny Carey have been using hybrid elements for over 25 years, the technology on offer now is more appealing than ever. The devices are cheaper and easier to transport from gig to gig so it is definitely worth giving the hybrid concept a try.

Tip!

If you are interested in the hybrid concept check out these drummers:
Neil Peart (Rush)
Danny Carey (Tool)
Aaron Spears (Usher)
John Blackwell (Prince)
Andy Gangadeen (Jeff Beck)
Richard Spaven (Flying Lotus)
Larnell Lewis (Snarky Puppy)

Musicianship

Professionalism

'Professional' is an over-used term but nonetheless it conveys some important concepts. Essentially your work (whether or not you are being paid) should be beyond criticism. This covers technical and musical matters as previously discussed in this series, but also issues such as punctuality and general attitude.

Be Punctual

Always assume that everyone else's time is valuable. This includes everyone you are working with, and applies most of all to studio time. Making people wait for you is always a bad idea, and almost guarantees a prejudice against working with you again, even if your performance is stellar. Make sure you allow plenty of time for unloading and setting up in time for the stated start time of your session, rehearsal or gig, and allow extra time for traffic delays, parking or other unforeseen eventualities.

If you know at the time of booking that things might be a little tight on the day (for example if you have other work that finishes with only just enough time to spare), make sure that your client knows about this and is still happy to book you on this basis. You may be able to arrange to have gear set up and waiting for you or to have someone else soundcheck your instruments, for example.

Be Prepared

Make sure that you are fully prepared for the work. For sight-reading gigs and sessions, even the most confident readers often ask to see parts in advance if possible. This can help you avoid situations where you are asked to play impossible parts. A quick look should help you identify any areas that may cause problems, allowing you to raise them with the bandleader or producer in advance. This shows a willingness to put in extra work and thought into getting things right and making the gig or session successful. Not all arrangers write perfect drums parts, and some parts simply require work in advance. There is no shame in admitting this.

For many gigs, you may have to learn songs by ear rather than reading. If this is stated at the outset, it is an integral part of the work you have taken on and should not be resented. Any additional work you can do at this stage to familiarise yourself with the artist and style will make the gig easier and more enjoyable. If you demonstrate a thorough understanding of the style and empathy for the artist, you are much more likely to get more work than if you just turn up and play the notes.

Be Committed

It is important to show commitment to your work at all times. Recording an album or playing a gig might be just another day in the office for you but the biggest day in the career of the artist you are working for. Conveying an honest feeling of commitment will work in your favour when clients are considering whether to book you again.

Although music is a profession and professionals in any field should be paid properly, it is important that clients don't think you are only there for the money. There are so many musicians looking for work and willing to play for little or nothing, that if you seem negative, or seem to be watching the clock at all times, the client usually won't hesitate to try someone else.

Managing your diary as a musician can create difficult judgment calls on a daily basis, assuming of course that you are in demand. When accepting an engagement, it is important to establish whether you will be allowed to find a substitute player if circumstances change, or if the client regards the booking as set in stone. Usually, it is better in the long run to take the attitude that 'a booking is a booking': don't let a client down in order to accept a slightly more lucrative gig. Even if you find someone else to take your place, that person may get every call from that client in the future and you will lose out in the long run. Of course, there are some situations where this becomes untenable, for example if you are offered a long tour and it clashes with a single gig. In these situations it is important to put in as much work as possible into finding an acceptable substitute player yourself, and if necessary rehearse them or write parts for them. People will be more likely to call you before others if they feel sure you won't let them down.

Attitude

Ensure that your attitude from the first moment of dealing with the client is always professional, positive and sensitive. If you have doubts about anything you can always ask questions, however busy music producers usually just want session musicians that come in prepared, do the job efficiently and quickly and leave so that they can continue with their project.

It is important also to be humble and show appreciation and respect for colleagues although they might be direct competitors. Nobody likes someone who puts others down, and it is not a good long term strategy – so focus on doing the best job you can, be flexible, be positive and be accommodating.

Getting Paid

Even if you decided to play because you just love music, beyond a certain level music is a job and you should be paid for your work.

The fee for each job will depend on many factors and should be agreed (ideally in writing) before you commit to the job. You can ask your contact when you will be paid and what details you will need in order to produce an invoice. In general, you will invoice the client and receive payment within an agreed period of time. Investigate the laws that apply in your country – you may need to invoke these as a last resort in the event of non-payment.

If you have a musician's trade union in your country, it might be a good idea to join it or least find out what type of support they can offer you. Usually, they offer legal advice and representation in the event of a dispute or non-payment. Remember that pursuing payments this way will usually be impossible unless you have a written contract, or at least very clear written communication with your client.

Royalties vs. Buy-Out

Royalty payments are a way of sharing the profits from a recording or other artistic product. Generally, there will be an agreement to pay you a certain percentage of profits, which are usually calculated after other fixed costs have been met. 'Proper' recording contracts with major record labels are usually based on royalties; further down the scale, you should be aware that people may offer royalties because they cannot afford a reasonable up-front fee, even though they have no expectation of making a profit. In this situation it may be preferable to negotiate a small fee, but it can be a difficult judgment.

Recording work may be paid in various ways:

- Buy-out: This means you get paid for the job and nothing thereafter. You agree to transfer all copyright in your work in return for a single fixed fee.
- Fee plus royalties: This means that there will be a fee for the job plus some royalties. If the album recording becomes successful you might earn some more money from it in the following years.
- Royalties only: This means that you will not be paid for the job but receive royalties instead. Therefore, you are taking a gamble as you will receive nothing if the recording is unsuccessful.
- Payment plus residuals: This arrangement is mainly used for film and TV music. You receive a buy-out fee for your work, but this only covers a single end product, with further fees for additional products. For example: you receive a payment based on a cinema release, but an additional fee if the film is shown on TV or released on DVD.

All this can be confusing, and if you feel that there may be a lot at stake you should consult an expert.

Tip!

As long as your skills and preparation are strong, it is your attitude that will determine how much work you get. The busiest session and live musicians are not always the best players, but the ones that are flexible and easy to work with.

Soloing

It is important to understand the framework of the solo so you can perform it in the most musical way.

Soloing is not about being perfect, it is about expressing who you are in relation to the music played. Let's look at some popular scenarios where drummers are asked to solo.

The Framework

Open solo: In this type of solo, there is no need to hold a consistent pulse or follow any form. The drummer is allowed total freedom of expression and leads the listener on a journey. Historically solos of this type used to be relatively long, leading to these being relatively rare in modern music. Open drum solos were very popular in seventies rock. 'Moby Dick' by Led Zeppelin (John Bonham) and 'Toad' by Cream (Ginger Baker) are classic examples of this type of solo. In many cases open solos start after part of the song has been played and afterwards the drummer will count the band in to play the rest of the song.

Soloing over a form: There is much more chance of you getting an opportunity to solo over a certain form than having an open solo on a weekly basis. This concept is popular in jazz, as jazz tunes usually have a melody (also known as the head) and a structure that can be followed by all players during the solos. Soloing over a form is a very important skill that requires practice. Apart from keeping to the form and maintaining the pulse we need to develop the ability to relate our solo to the music that is played. Finding a rhythmic or melodic motif from the song to develop is always a good way to start.

Trading fours: This means that the drummer solos for four bars and then another band member solos for four bars and so on. This concept is also known as question and answer. Trading fours can also be practised with another drummer or a programmed loop. Remember that you do not have to imitate what you hear but can actually voice your own 'thoughts' and 'opinions' of what was said (or played) by the other musician. Sometimes, this will mean repeating parts of what was said, saying something in the same style or saying something completely different. Use the example below in order to understand this concept better.

1

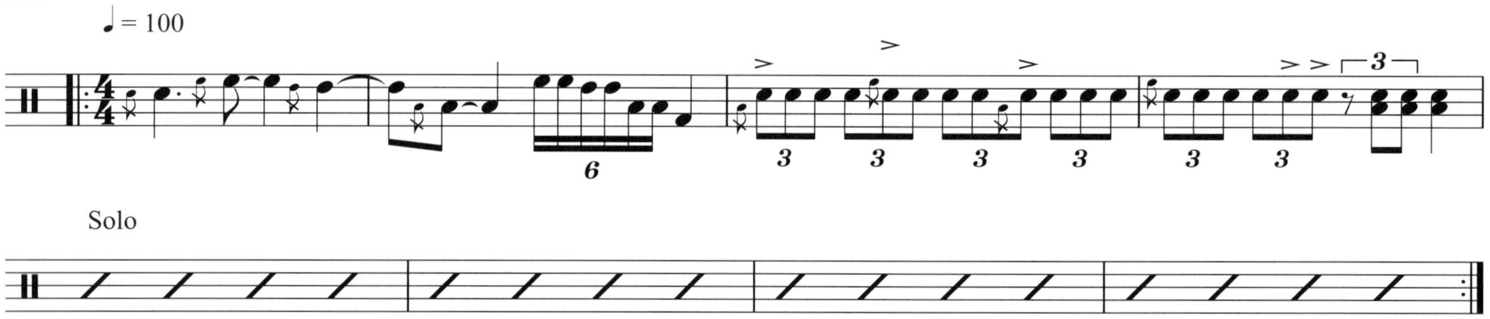

Soloing on a riff: This is possibly the most common type of drum solo in music today, and is similar to soloing over a form but easier as the riff is much shorter and simpler to follow. The riff can be played by live musicians, or even a drum loop or drum machine. The length of these solos will vary according to the music. Mostly, these solos are ended on cue. This means that the band members will repeat the solo section constantly until the drummer signals to move on. Remember that your solo is supposed to serve the music and not just provide a platform for you to show off your most recent rudiment or stick trick.

If you have a band where drum solos are appropriate and appreciated by the other members you are one lucky drummer, but most drummers only get to solo as part of their practice and often use a metronome, drum machine or loop. In **Ex. 2** the rhythm of the riff is indicated in the notation for you to follow.

Try programming this rhythm into your drum machine and set it to loop so you can practise soloing over it. If you want to push yourself further, try writing new ideas for riffs and solo over them. Then, try to do this process again but vary the time signature.

2 ♩ = 100

Soloing over an ostinato: In a similar way, a riff can be created by playing a repetitive foot pattern known as an ostinato. You can improvise with your hands while holding the ostinato with the feet. This concept is a very popular practice tool as it strengthens four-way coordination as well as soloing skills.

3 ♩ = 100

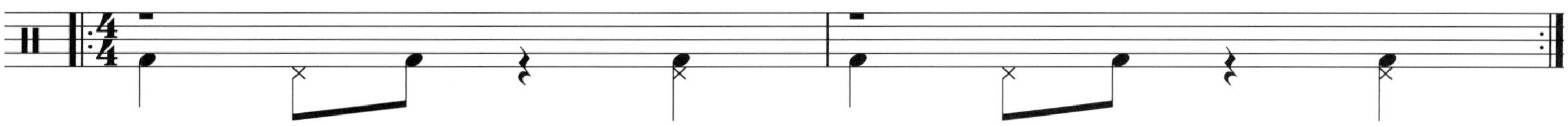

Internal clock: Understanding the concepts of soloing and practising them repeatedly will make you a better soloist, but ultimately it is your sense of time that will determine how convincing your phrases sound and how natural and fluent your solos are. In **Ex. 4** there are four bars for you to improvise on. Use a drum machine and programme two bars of metronome and two bars of silence (the metronome continues to count the beats but is not heard). This way you need to carry on soloing and also feel where the pulse is. When the click comes back in, you will know if you are on track or need to adjust. Carry on practising this until it feels comfortable and accurate, then change the tempo and try again. Finally, create different tracks with longer and longer sections without a click. The longer you are able to perform your solo in time without the click, the better your internal clock.

1 ♩ = 100

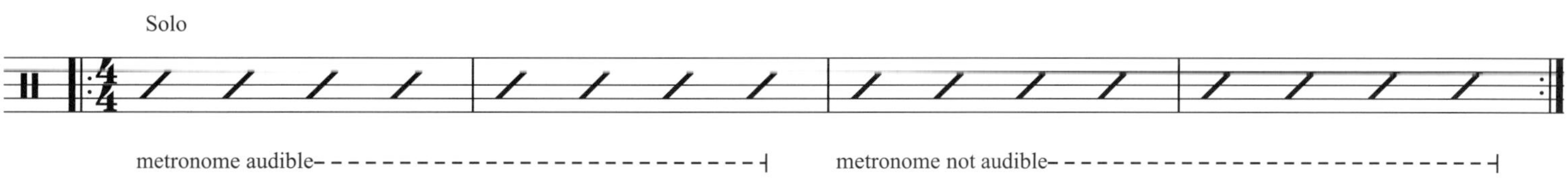

Creating and Allowing Space

Soloing is like having a conversation. With this in mind, you must realise that playing all the ideas, rudiments and exercises you know as fast as you can in one solo will not produce your best musical work. As with any conversation, you should speak and then listen. Short rests or breaks between phrases are necessary – do not be afraid of creating and allowing space. The space that you create will help you shape your musical phrases better and will be an integral part of your sound. The concept of space is one of the most important concepts in this series. Understanding and integrating it into your playing will help you unlock the secrets of drumming and become a better musician overall. Check out Joe Morello's drum solo on the track 'Take Five' by Dave Brubeck to understand the concept of space in a solo.

Ear Training

Play each audio track without looking at the examples below.

After a count-in of four clicks, the two-bar backing is played four times. For the first and third times, listen to the rhythms played. For the second and fourth times, try to play them back yourself.

Finally, refer to the notation below to check whether you recognised the time signature, played back the exercise accurately and understand how it is written.

Rhythms

1

2

3

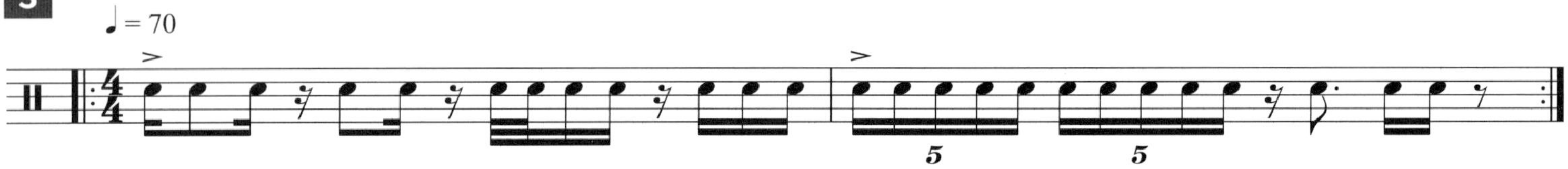

The following three exercises use the same rhythms as those above but with the toms as well as the snare drum. The practice concept is the same.

4

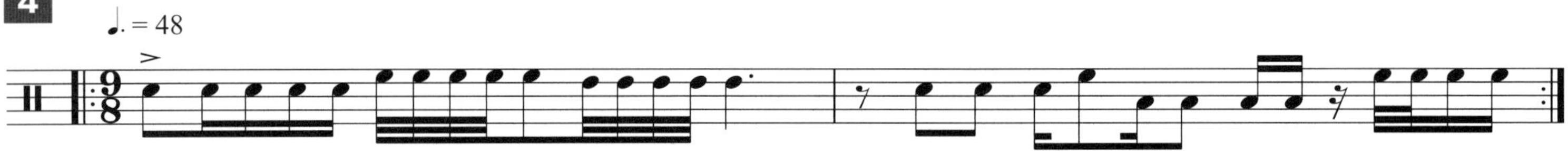

5

6

Grooves

You will notice that **Exercises 1–3** are groove based. This means that more parts of the drum kit will be used. This requires secure aural understanding as you will not only have to recognise the rhythms but also the drum voices that are being played.

As explained previously, the backing track will play four times and you should attempt to play back during the second and fourth plays. We will focus on $\frac{4}{4}$ cut time, $\frac{9}{8}$ and $\frac{13}{16}$ in these grooves, but feel free to create your own exercises in other time signatures too.

1

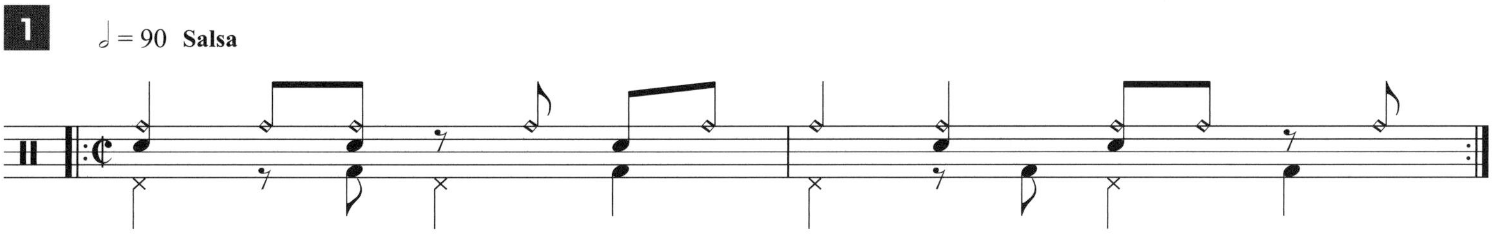

2

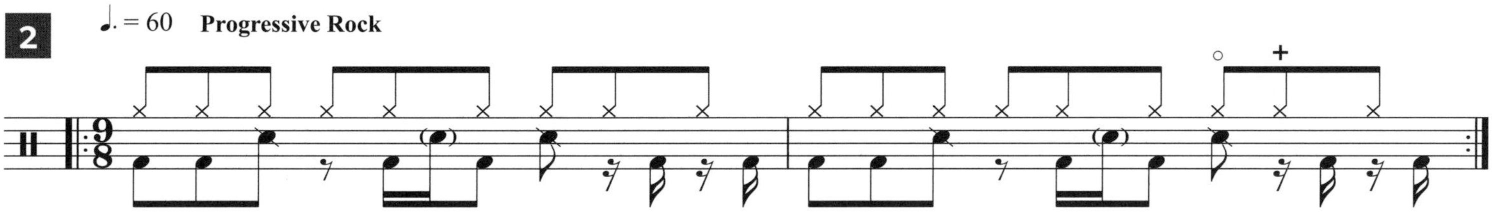

3

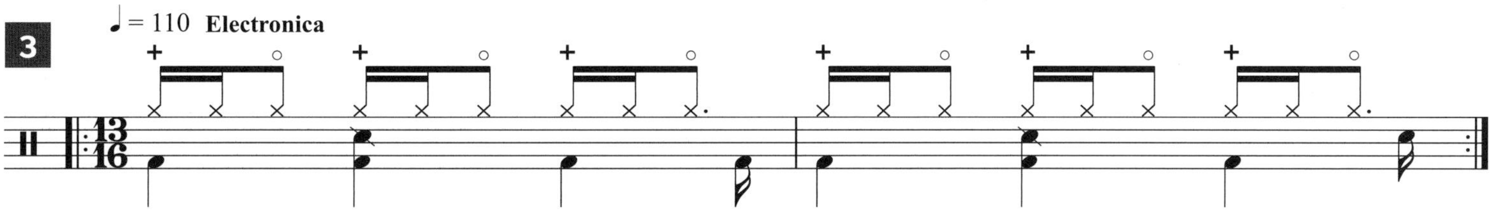

Now, let's take two-bar grooves and place a two beat fill at the end of the phrase. See if you can identify all the detail and play them back with conviction.

4

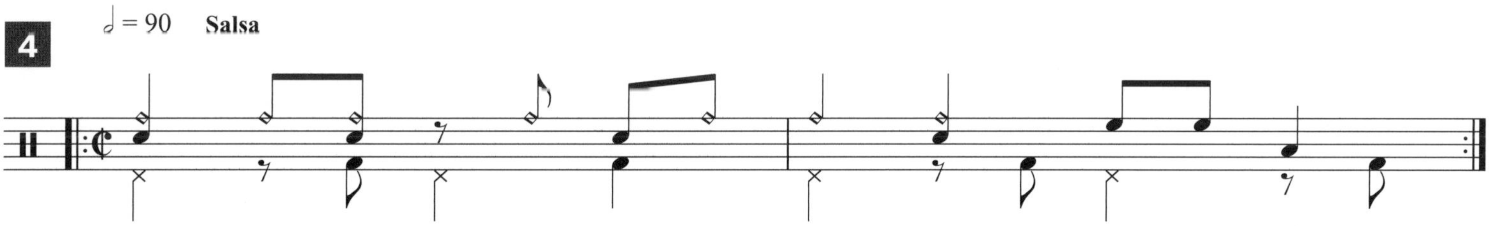

5

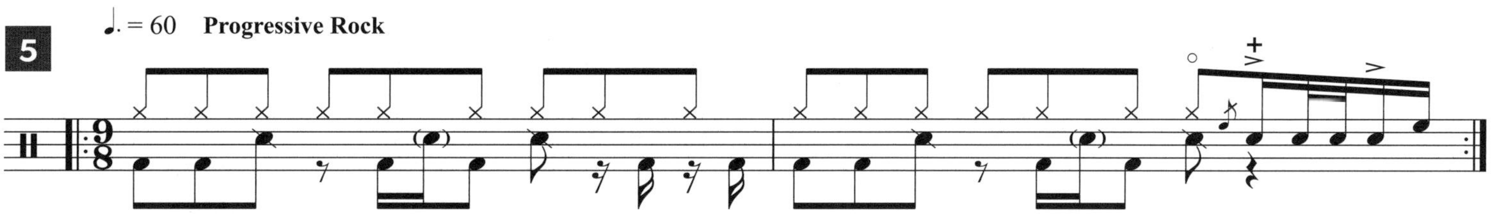

6

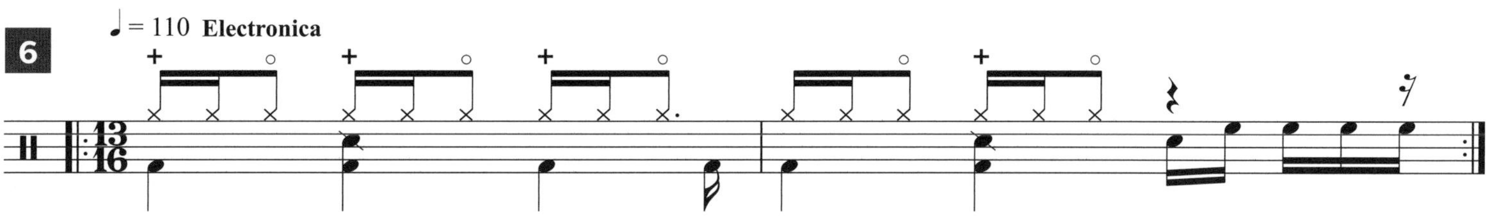

Inspirational Drummers

Vinnie Colaiuta

Vinnie Colaiuta is one of the most recorded drummers in history, with a discography of over 500 studio albums. Colaiuta is known for his musical versatility and ability to play any style of music convincingly. His first big break was in 1976 when he joined the Christopher Morris band after attending Berklee College of Music in Boston. At the age of 22 he successfully auditioned for the Frank Zappa band and recorded the classic albums *Tinseltown Rebellion*, *Joe's Garage* and *Shut Up 'n Play Yer Guitar*. After leaving Zappa, Colaiuta worked with many famous rock and pop artists including Joni Mitchell, Barbra Streisand, Jeff Beck, Chaka Khan and Joe Satriani as well as jazz musicians such as Chick Corea, Herbie Hancock and Robben Ford.

In 1990 Colaiuta joined the band of international superstar Sting and remained a permanent member for seven years. His musical and ground-breaking drumming with Sting can be heard on the studio albums *Ten Summoner's Tales*, *Mercury Falling* and some songs on *Brand New Day* and *Sacred Love*. The exposure he gained during his time with Sting made him an even bigger star and a global drumming phenomenon. Colaiuta re-joined Sting in 2011 and to date still performs live to the pleasure of many of his fans. Colaiuta has also kept recording constantly with various artists, achieving one of the most extensive studio credit lists of any drummer in the world.

During his career Colaiuta has worked with various drum and cymbal manufacturers. He most notably developed the A Custom range of cymbals with Zildjian in the 1990 and the re-vamped 602 series with Paiste in 2012. There is also a signature snare drum developed for him by Yamaha and a complete signature drum kit by Gretsch. Colaiuta is currently using Heuer drums, Paiste cymbals and Vic Firth sticks.

Recommended Listening

'Joe's Garage' (Zappa)
'Seven Days' (Sting)
'Behind the Veil' (Jeff Beck)

Jojo Mayer

Jojo Mayer is one of the most innovative modern drummers in the world. Mixing his jazz background with electronic music he created a unique style of drumming that blends jazz, drum and bass and jungle. Mayer is also known for his ability to play programmed electronic beats on the acoustic drum kit, a technique that he calls 'reverse engineering'.

Mayer's first break came at the age of 18 when he joined the Monty Alexander group. He then carried on playing with various jazz artists such as Dizzy Gillespie and Nina Simone until he started developing the electronic side of his playing. In 1997 Mayer founded the live electronica trio Nerve. This outfit allowed him to explore new drumming directions and perform his 'reverse engineered' beats to the New York crowds on a weekly basis. These popular club nights, known as Prohibited Beatz, ran for about five years. At the same time, Mayer also became involved in education and started demonstrating his innovative approach during clinics and drum festival appearances with Nerve.

Playing programmed beats on the acoustic drum kit involves the use of advanced hand and foot techniques. Mayer use a combination of rebound techniques such as the heel-toe technique with the bass drum, the Moeller stroke with the hands and the famous push pull Technique. These allow him to play accurate and very fast strokes using the natural rebound of the stick. In 2008 Mayer released *Secret Weapons for the Modern Drummer*, an important educational DVD that clearly explains the physics of drumming and how to integrate such advanced techniques into your approach to the instrument. It is still regarded as one of the best drum technique DVDs ever released. Mayer plays Sonor drums and Sabian cymbals. With Sabian he created two successful lines of cymbals, the Vault Fierce series and the AAX Omni series.

Recommended Listening

'Tetrastigm' (Nerve)
'Surfin'' (Album: *Elevator Dubs*)
'Loot' (Nerve)

Neil Peart

Neil Peart is a Canadian musician and author best known as the drummer and lyricist for the progressive rock band Rush. Although Peart is considered to be one of the best rock drummers in the world, his unique style actually combines hard rock with components of jazz. He was heavily influenced by rock drummers such as John Bonham and Keith Moon and jazz drummers including Gene Krupa and Buddy Rich.

Peart joined Rush in 1974 after the release of their debut album. The band grew in popularity and became famous for complex compositions mixed with eclectic lyrics. Rush have continued to record, tour and inspire generations of musicians worldwide.
Peart's drum setup has continuously evolved during his career and he has experimented with adding many percussion instruments to the acoustic drum kit. These include bells, chimes, crotales, timbales, timpani, gong, temple blocks and cowbells. He has also used electronic drums and triggers in his setup since 1984. Most recently, Peart has been using an elaborate 360-degree drum kit, with a large acoustic set in front and electronic drums to the rear.

Apart from being the main lyricist for Rush, Peart is the author of five non-fiction books chronicling his personal development on journeys to Cameroon, Brazil, North America and Europe.

Recommended Listening

'YYZ'
'Tom Sawyer'
'Spirit of Radio'

Style Focus: Progressive Rock

Odd Time Signatures

Odd time signatures are fundamental to much progressive rock. By now you should already feel confident playing many odd time signatures. Remember that the more you play and practise in odd time signatures the more comfortable they will feel. In this lesson we will focus on creative ways of developing odd time signatures in depth. Ultimately it all comes down to numbers which can be divided, subdivided, displaced and grouped in many ways to achieve different rhythmic and musical results.

Displacement

This is one of the most effective concepts of progressive rock music and drumming. In **Ex. 1** we have a simple eighth note rock beat. In the second bar we displace the bass drum and snare patterns forwards by one eighth note. In **Ex. 2** we displace the bass drum and snare patterns backwards by a sixteenth note. Groove displacements can be effective in other styles of music, even as an alternative to fills.

1

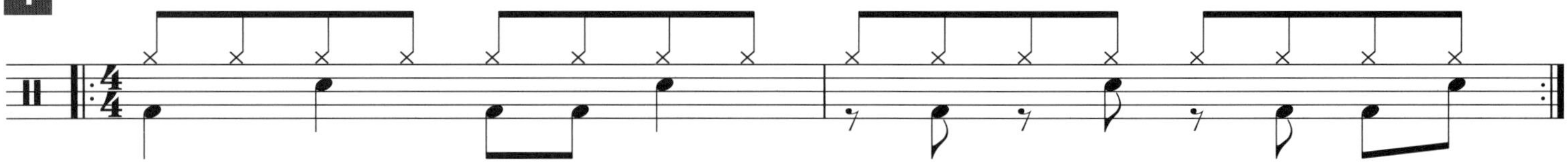

2

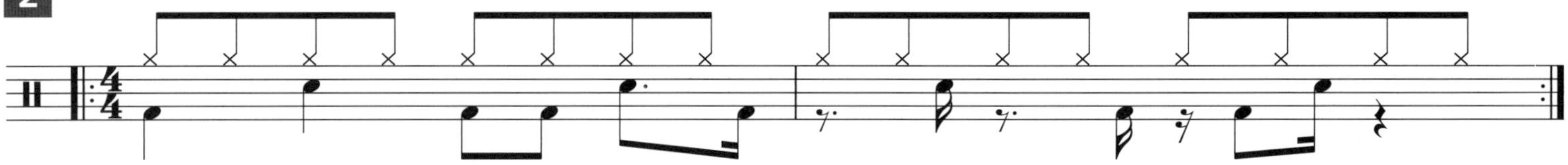

Advanced Displacement

We can take this concept further and use more advanced displacements with odd time signatures. This includes changing one pattern and keeping the other consistent (also known as overriding). The groove is in $\frac{5}{8}$ and the overriding pattern is played on the hi-hat.

3

Eighth note override

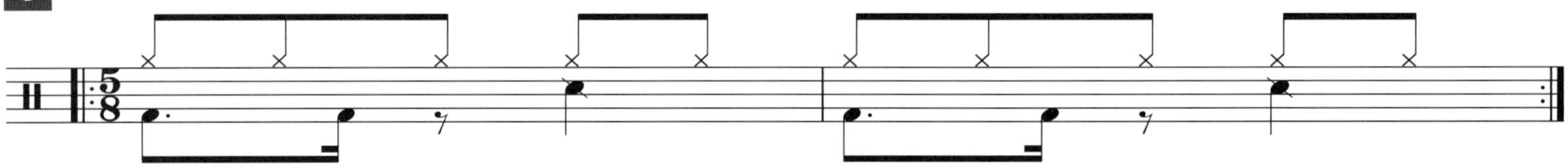

4

Quarter note override

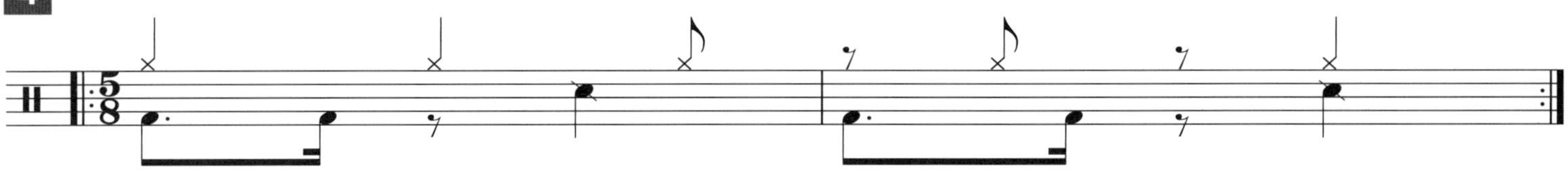

5

Dotted eighth note override

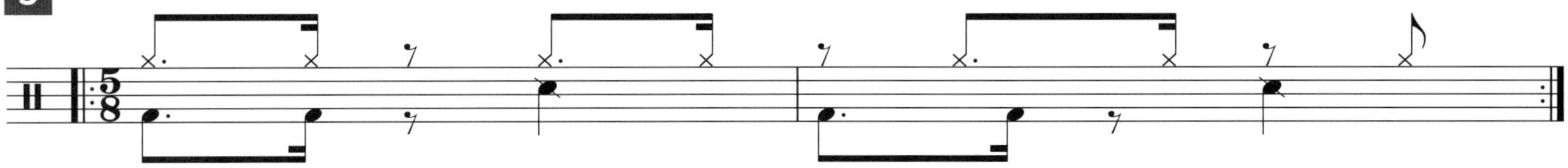

Metric Modulation

Metric modulation, also known as rhythmic manipulation and rhythmic illusion, is another useful concept in progressive rock drumming, and affects the listener by creating the feeling of a tempo change. First, play **Ex. 1** (a standard 12/8 groove).

Then try **Ex. 2** where the illusion of an implied faster tempo is created and **Ex. 3** where a slower one is created. When you can play these three grooves, try moving between them consistently until this feels natural. Moving forward, you should easily be able to create many variations of this concept and apply it to what you already know.

1

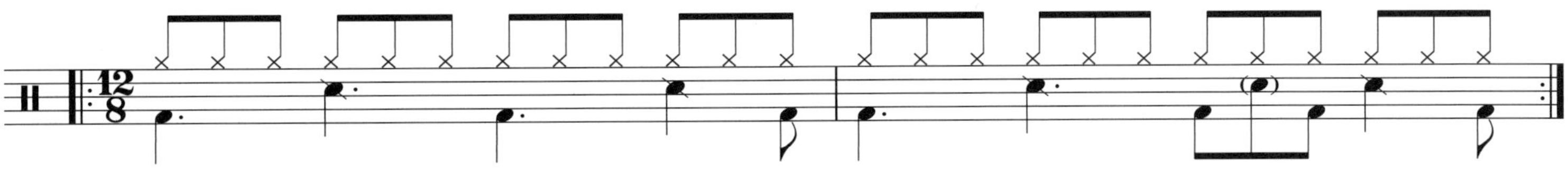

2

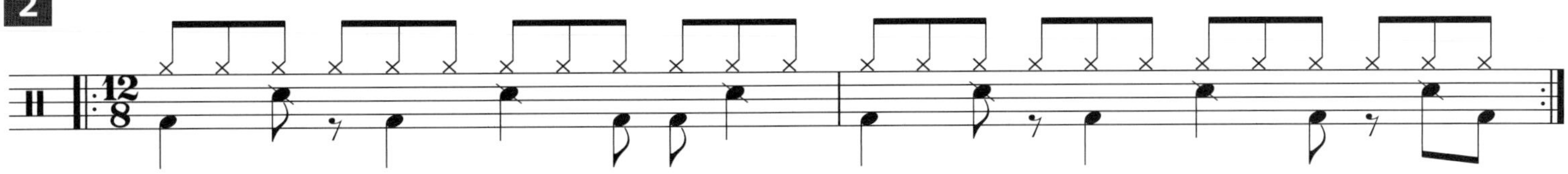

3

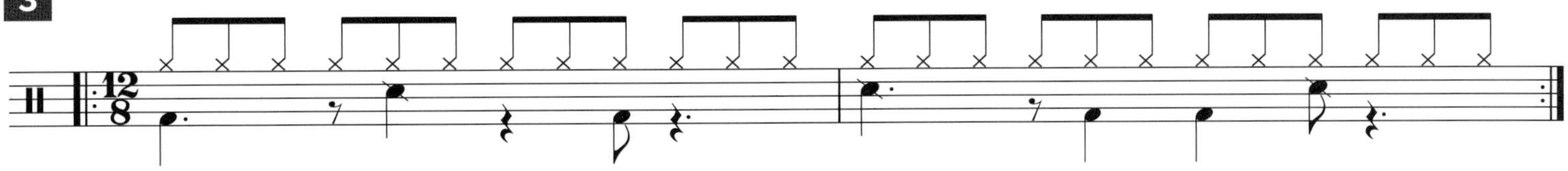

Ex. 4 uses the same concept in an improvised phrase that can be used as a fill or in a solo.

4

Being in Control

The most important element of all the concepts presented here is to understand exactly what effect you are trying to create and being in control of the change. This mainly means that you should be able to bring the displacement or modulation back with conviction.

Do not stay in the implied rhythm for too long as this will reduce its effect and confuse the listener as well as other players.

Piece Preparation: 'Time Machine'

This is a progressive rock piece in the style of Neil Peart, Gavin Harrison and Bill Bruford. The backing track of 'Time Machine' can be downloaded for free from **www.vvinner.com/downloads**.

A Intro

The challenging intro groove consists of a few fundamental elements of progressive rock drumming: odd time signatures, rhythmic displacement, rhythmic manipulation and subdivisions.

The first groove is notated in $\frac{5}{4}$ but if you look at the first two bars as one unit and examine the bass drum and snare pattern, you will see that the combined beats in these two bars (10 beats) are divided into 3, 4, and 3. **Ex. 1** will help you understand this clearly.

Once you have understood how to play the snare and bass drum pattern, including the changes from $\frac{5}{4}$ to $\frac{3}{4}$ you should progress to the crash cymbal pattern. This pattern may be difficult to coordinate at first but with counting and practise you will be able to achieve this impressive progressive rock groove. The crash cymbal pattern follows a quarter note forward displacement from bar 6. Once you understand the concept you will be able to play it with more conviction.

B Verse

The verse groove is in $\frac{7}{4}$. Pay close attention to the accented and non-accented hi-hats as this will give the groove a unique flow. If you want to stretch your coordination skills try practising this $\frac{7}{4}$ groove with off-beat accents on the hi-hat, or even with alternating accents as notated in **Ex 2**.

One of the main challenges of this groove is playing the three consecutive ghost notes on the snare. Although these can be played as rebounds, for maximum accuracy and balanced projection try using controlled taps as explained in the Gladstone Technique in p. 6. Practising controlled taps with both hands on a regular basis will significantly develop your stick control and sensitivity on the kit.

When working on this groove also remember to focus on the rim shot sound, the accuracy of the bass drum and the flow of $\frac{7}{4}$.

C Chorus

In the chorus the groove changes to $\frac{4}{4}$ but one of the backbeat snares in each bar is played a sixteenth note earlier than usual. In addition the hi-hat plays consistent eighth notes while the leading hand pattern alternates between the ride cymbal and the bell of the ride (**Ex. 3**). Having mastered this four-way coordination groove, try to add ghost note snares to create intensity.

D Guitar Solo

The groove in the guitar solo is the same as the verse section but here you have the opportunity to develop the groove according to your understanding of the style and your personal taste. Refer back to *Style Focus: Progressive Rock* (p. 88) and plan how you will implement stylistic concepts into this development section. Do not forget that this section leads into the drum solo, so you may wish to plant seeds that will grow further in the following section which is the drum solo.

E Drum Solo

Soloing in odd time signatures is vital for progressive rock drummers. I suggest initially practising your favourite drum licks or phrases with a $\frac{7}{4}$ metronome. Find ways of utilising what you already know and adapting it to the new time signature. Once you feel more comfortable playing and soloing in this odd time signature you will naturally start creating interesting phrases that imply the $\frac{7}{4}$ time, or phrases that create a rhythmic illusion of a different time signature over $\frac{7}{4}$. For example, if we take two bars of $\frac{7}{4}$ we have 14 quarter note beats. This number can be divided in endless ways but let's look at a reasonably simple one: 4, 4, 4 and 2 (**Ex. 4**). Practising concepts like this in odd time signatures will give you command of the pulse and confidence to create rhythmic manipulations for the listener during your drum solo.

F Coda

The coda section begins with the same groove as the intro. After four bars of $\frac{5}{4}$ the time signature changes to $\frac{2}{4}$ which leads to the final hit in bar 55. Ensure that you play crash cymbal and bass drum at the beginning of this bar with conviction. If you want to experiment with new cymbal sounds this is a great opportunity to do so. You can try to play the crash cymbal pattern on another appropriate cymbal, the china cymbal. The 'stack' is another device that can be used here: several cymbals stacked together in order to achieve a new and unique sound. There are no rules. Experiment with the cymbals you have until you find sounds that you like.

If you want to challenge yourself further, play the bass drum and snare patterns in $\frac{5}{4}$ and change the cymbal pattern to overriding quarter notes, dotted eighth notes or even quarter note triplets. The quarter note overriding is shown in **Ex. 5**.

Never settle for just playing what is written. Push yourself, find ways to inspire yourself and strive to continue to improve all the time. Use your taste and stylistic knowledge to judge what works best for the music you are playing.

1

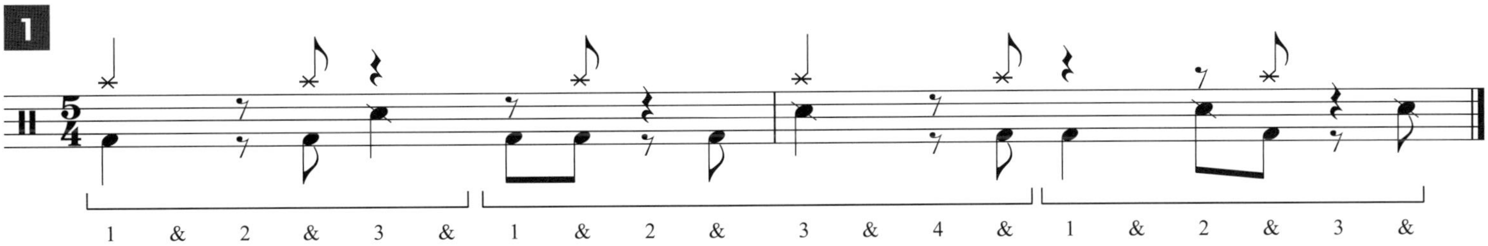

2

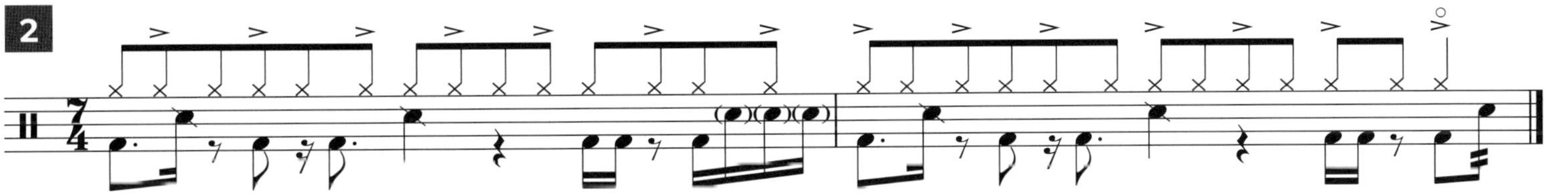

3

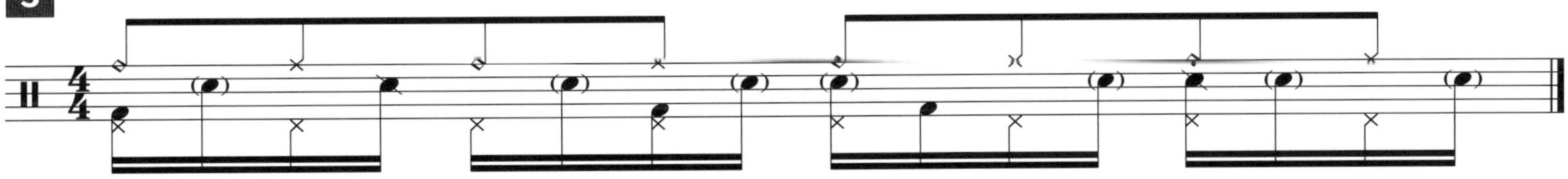

4

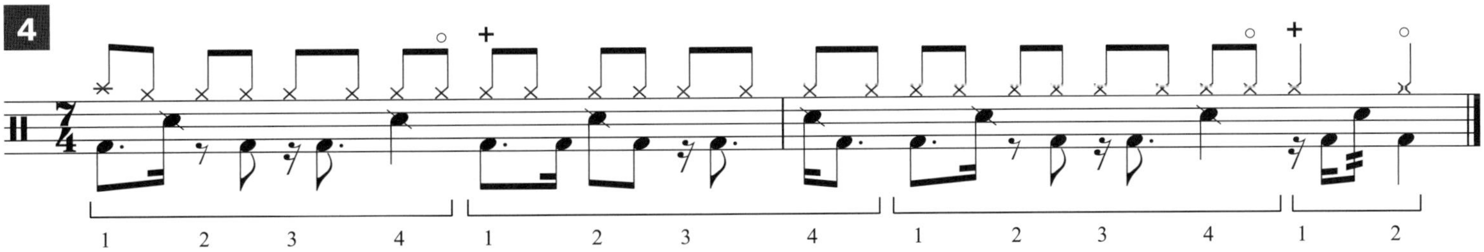

5

'Time Machine'

15
17
C
19 (50)
21 (52)
23 (54)
25 (56)

To Coda
27 (58)
3/16
29
5/4
31
3/4
6
D
Guitar Solo
34
7/4
36
Develop
38

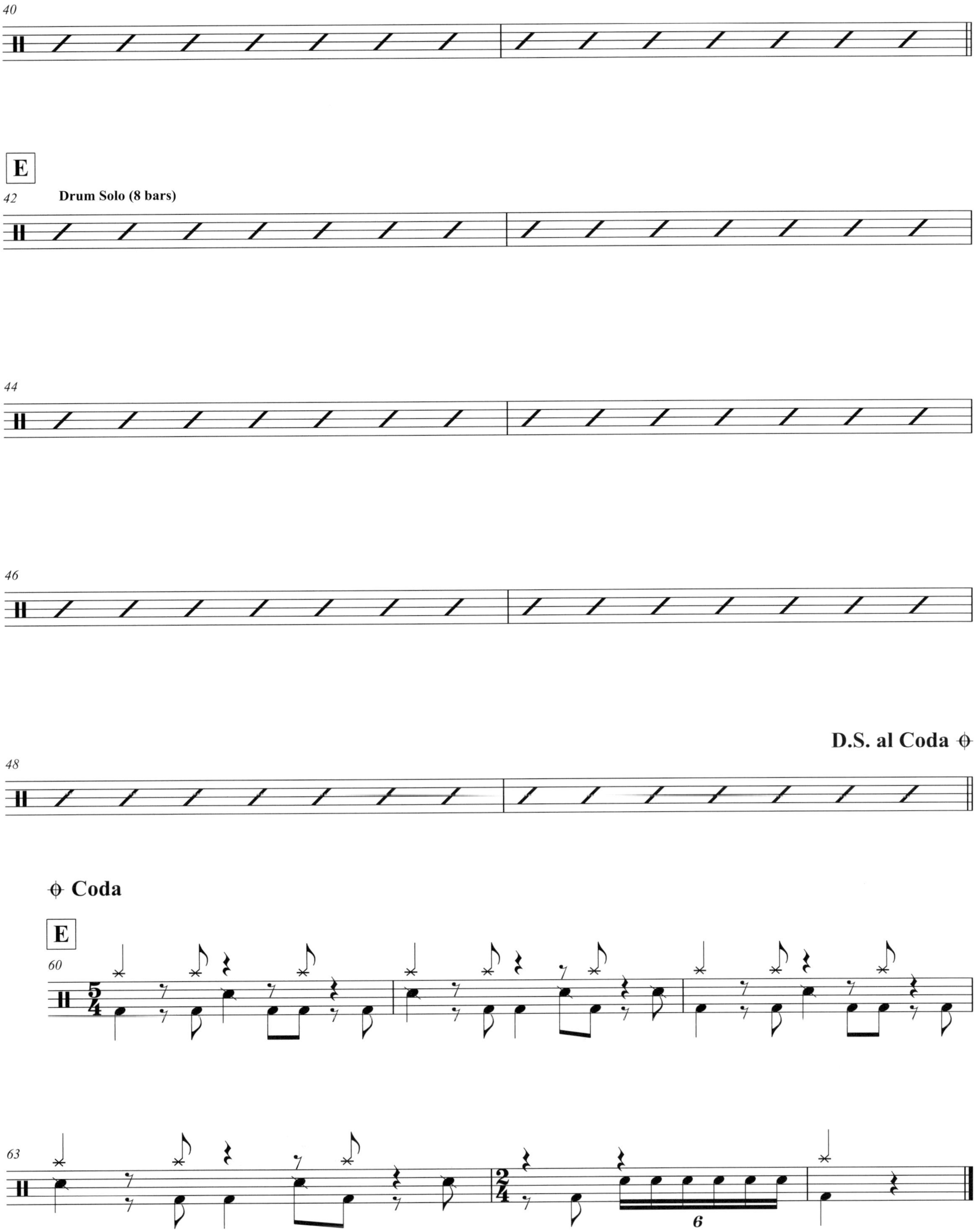
40
E
42
Drum Solo (8 bars)
44
46
D.S. al Coda
48
Coda
E
60
63
6

About the Author

Noam Lederman is a musician, educator and author based in the UK. He has built a successful music career combining performance and writing. He has written more than 100 music publications that have sold over a million copies worldwide.

Noam has a postgraduate degree in Jazz from the Guildhall School of Music and Drama. He has worked with renowned musicians such as Billy Cobham, Dave Liebman, Kenny Wheeler, Corinne Bailey Rae, State of Bengal, Mark Hill and Trevor Horn.

Noam has performed at many music festivals including Womad, Glastonbury, Reading and Sonar as well as appearing on MTV. He regularly performs at various events across the globe, thus continuing to develop his instrumental skills.

After being a music examiner for many years, in 2009 Noam was appointed Chief Examiner for the international music board Rockschool. In 2014 Noam founded the company VVinner Music which provides high quality educational products and services to music institutions.

In April 2015 Noam was appointed as the Principal of The Academy of Rock - an award winning franchise of music schools in Asia.

Noam continues to inspire and educate as an academic consultant working with music institutions, schools and teachers worldwide to raise their standards and be the best in their field.

For more information or if you wish to contact the author please visit **www.noamlederman.com**.

Vinner

VVinner Music is one of the most exciting and vibrant companies in the music education sector providing high quality educational products and offering support to academic institutions across the globe.

Established in 2014 by a professional musician with a passion for education and an entrepreneur with a vision, with two headquarters (Singapore and London), we can work with anyone, anywhere, either in person or remotely.

VVinner Music publishes specialist music education books. In 2016 VVinner released a ground-breaking series of tuition books for guitar and drums titled *Unlocking the Secrets*. This series has been created to complement one-to-one tuition, and to assist both teachers and students.

VVinner Music offers academic consultation to institutions and schools, utilising our in-house expertise and skills in the area of music education. Services include re-standardising teaching methods, checking for consistency of marking, reviewing, advising and re-writing teaching methods, while adhering to high quality and international standards.

VVinner Music provides bespoke training for those working in the music education sector. We can tailor training programmes for tutors and teachers to help them achieve better exam results and increase their level of skill.

VVinner Music is committed to music education for children around the world and is currently developing groundbreaking music programmes for children.

Our mission is to make music education and learning accessible to all ages, and to connect musicians across the globe, thus creating a network of like minded individuals who all have one passion in life – MUSIC!

For more information, please visit **www.vvinner.com**

Vinner

LEARN - CREATE - CONNECT